HOW TO
HOOK and
LAUNCH

Traction Mods for Street & Strip

Dick Miller

S·A DESIGN

CarTech®

CarTech®

CarTech®, Inc.
838 Lake Street South
Forest Lake, MN 55025
Phone: 651-277-1200 or 800-551-4754
Fax: 651-277-1203
www.cartechbooks.com

Edit by Scott Parkhurst
Layout by Monica Seiberlich

ISBN 978-1-61325-519-3
Item No. SA195P

Library of Congress Cataloging-in-Publication Data

Miller, Dick,
How to hook and launch : traction mods for street & strip / by Dick Miller.
    p. cm. – (S-A design)
  ISBN 978-1-934709-35-1
1. Dragsters–Design and construction. 2. Automobiles–Springs and suspension. 3. Automobiles–Customizing. I. Title.
  TL236.2.M55 2012
  629.28'72–dc23
                    2011049287

Written, edited, and designed in the U.S.A.
Printed in the U.S.A.

Title Page:

Post-1979 Ford Mustangs (and all other Fox-chassis Ford vehicles) used a MacPherson-strut front suspension with great success. They are very popular drag cars due to their light weight and rear-wheel-drive design. (Photo by Eric McClellan)

Back Cover Photos

Top:

This is Dan Zrust in a 1968 Plymouth Barracuda. The car competes in the notoriously tough Super Stock ranks and is powered by the venerable 426-ci Chrysler Hemi engine. This shot was taken at the 2009 NHRA U.S. Nationals in Indianapolis, Indiana.

Middle:

A bit too much rotation and you're on the back bumper. Not only is energy being used to push this car rearward on this particular launch, but how aerodynamic do you figure this is? A slight adjustment is all it takes to make this better, and since this was during time trials it was the right time to experiment.

Bottom:

Chuck Lipka's 1941 Willys Gasser runs a tubular front axle with a well-designed cross-steer setup. You can also see top-quality front tires and modern disc brakes. The front suspension maintains the vintage look while being safer overall.

DISTRIBUTION BY:

Europe
PGUK
63 Hatton Garden
London EC1N 8LE, England
Phone: 020 7061 1980 • Fax: 020 7242 3725

Australia
Renniks Publications Ltd.
3/37-39 Green Street
Banksmeadow, NSW 2109, Australia
Phone: 2 9695 7055 • Fax: 2 9695 7355

CONTENTS

DEDICATION

To my dad, Earle Miller, and my brother-in-law, Clete LaFollette. My dad helped promote my interest in fast cars, which over the years I turned into a "need for speed." Clete was instrumental in helping me to develop a self-taught interest in modifying cars for even faster speeds. Clete was a inspiration to me who taught me if you are going to do a job it must be done right no matter how long it takes and if it's not done right, it's not done.

ACKNOWLEDGMENTS

Most of the information in this book is a accumulation of my 40-plus years of drag racing experience and suspension designing. I thank God for allowing me to live the life I have been able to live and my wife and daughters for putting up with me.

A very special thanks goes to Gene McMannis for his first-hand information and for the effort he put forth in assembling the descriptions of the beginning of not only drag racing but his subsequent involvement and evolution of the drag racing tires that we know today.

Thanks to John Calvert for his explanation of cars with rear leaf springs and what it takes to make them work.

I would like to thank Scott Parkhurst and CarTech, Inc. for giving me the opportunity to author this book and pass on my extensive experience.

It seems as I get older more and more of the people that I first started drag racing with have passed on. I think more efforts like this need to be made to get some of this information recorded before it is also gone.

ABOUT THE AUTHOR

Already having an occupation when I graduated from high school I saw no need to go to college. I was cutting meat in a grocery store. I eventually worked my way up to be a journeyman meat cutter for the A&P Tea Company. After several years of working in 33 degree F temperatures, I decided to quit and go to a computer programming school. With that training, I went to work for the Budd Company. Fourteen years later the plant closed and I was out of work. I started teaching computer classes to the inmates at the Southern Michigan Prison in Jackson, Michigan. From there, I went to work for EDS in Texas, doing computer training at Oldsmobile's main headquarters in Lansing, Michigan. A year later I started my own computer software business, creating software for automotive parts suppliers.

With my knowledge of Oldsmobiles, and requests from others to build traditional Oldsmobile engines for them, I opened Dick Miller Racing in 1992. The business was devoted to selling parts and providing expert technical advice to other Olds enthusiasts. Wanting to branch out even further (using my already developed knowledge of race car suspensions) I launched a suspension line for my beloved GM cars in 1996, and then expanded to include Ford vehicles soon after.

Over the past 45 years, I have had several race-only cars, including a tube-chassis-equipped, four-link-suspended 1991 Olds Cutlass running as quick as 8.50-second passes in the quarter-mile at over 160 mph. I also ran a traditional Olds V-8 powered car capable of 60-foot times in 1.22 seconds, built for me by Advanced Chassis in Antwerp, Ohio.

The first car I ever raced was a new 1964 Pontiac Catalina with a 389-ci Pontiac engine, a 4-speed manual transmission, and cheater slicks. I remember running time trials at Milan, Michigan, when they ran four-cars-wide at a time. I could often be found on the streets of Toledo, Ohio, racing from stoplight to stoplight in that Catalina. This same Pontiac later served as a family car, and sometimes I would remove the backseat and lay down a piece of plywood for the kids to play on as we traveled on vacations. Times sure have changed!

Dick Miller breaking in a 511-ci EFI Olds engine for an article in the August 2006 Hot Rod magazine.

March 2011 Dick Miller at Holly Springs Dragway with his one-owner, original-paint, original-interior, 1970 Cutlass W-31 he bought new in 1969.

I still have dreams of finding that car in an old barn, looking just like it was the day I sold it. In my early teen years, my parents took me to a "drag race" at an airport with a concrete launch pad. It was only about 60 feet long, and right where the concrete ended and the dirt started was a trench dug by the car's tires spinning as they left the concrete and tried to grip into the dirt. It was primitive, but still very exciting.

I have owned many Oldsmobile race cars since then. I still own the car featured on the front cover of this book—a 1970 Oldsmobile Cutlass S W-31. It was originally a small-block, 4-speed manual transmission car I bought new in the fall of 1969. I also removed the backseat of that car for a family trip to Colorado, where I drove it all the way to the top of Pikes Peak and back down with the kids on the floor in the backseat. While many cars had to stop at a brake-testing station halfway back down to let their brakes cool, my car (with the manual transmission) continued on, as downshifting kept me from riding the brakes as with cars with automatic transmissions.

In the 1970s, even with the best GM parts available, this car regularly broke the rear axle. Launching at 5,000 rpm with rear drag racing slicks installed, it broke an axle every other weekend.

I wanted to keep going quicker and eventually switched to a 455-ci Olds engine with a Turbo 350 automatic transmission. The big-block also proved to be more reliable than the high-winding small-block. Behind the torque of the 455 Olds, a Turbo 350 automatic transmission was simply not strong enough. I switched to a stronger Turbo 400. The big-block Olds/Turbo 400 car has run mid-10-second passes down the quarter-mile and reaches almost identical trap speeds in the eighth-mile that I did 40 years ago in the quarter-mile. All this while still being licensed, street legal, in full street trim, and weighing more than 3,800 pounds. I still race that same car and combination today—with much stronger and more reliable parts—and it needs very little regular maintenance. That doesn't mean I won't be working on the car if you see me at the track. I am continually researching, designing, and testing new parts and different combinations.

With my full-time parts business, I don't get to do much racing anymore. But in the winter of 2008 I decided to let a few things slide and entered my 1970 Cutlass S W-31 in the local 2009 points program foot-brake class where I started about 45 years ago. I was very pleased to win the points championship in Holly Springs, Mississippi. This was not my first championship. I have won numerous local, state, and national events throughout my racing years. I have an IHRA National Event trophy, as well as an NHRA Event trophy. I had another 1970 Cutlass that I set an IHRA record in (D/PSA class) back in the 1980s. I also raced a 1985 Olds Calais car for a short time with a 4 cylinder/front-wheel-drive automatic drivetrain, as well as a traditional rear-drive leaf-sprung 1974 Olds Omega with which I won the IHRA Northern Nationals in Milan, Michigan.

Dick Miller racing his 1970 W-31 at the 14th annual Oldsmobile Powered Nationals held every July at Summit Motorsports Park in Norwalk, Ohio.

INTRODUCTION

This book is designed to explain the principles of why Ford, GM, Chrysler, and AMC classic muscle cars act the way they do under hard acceleration, and how to make it better. Armed with this knowledge, you can maximize your car's traction. This gives you an advantage your competitor may not have. The book then explores the different rear suspensions (leaf springs, three links, and four-link), then front suspensions (solid axle, double A-arm, single A-arm, and torsion bar). I then discuss tires, tuning suspensions for maximum traction, and finally how to make your car more consistent and therefore more likely a winner.

Originally, rear-wheel-drive cars were designed with comfort, sta-

bility, and performance in mind. Today's incredible horsepower levels greatly exceed what factory suspensions were designed to handle.

When making any of the changes described in this book, you must also follow any and all necessary safety recommendations for the work you are accomplishing. Safety comes first, and you can never be safe enough.

As stated in the NHRA rule book: "Drag racing is a dangerous sport. There is no such thing as a guaranteed safe drag race. Drag racing always carries with it the risk of serious injury or death in any number of ways. This risk will always exist no matter how much everyone connected with drag racing tries to make our sport safer. Although the NHRA

works to promote and enhance the safety of the sport, there are no guarantees that such safety measures will guarantee or ensure safety. The participant always has the responsibility for the participants own safety, and by participating in drag racing, the participant accepts all risks of injury, whether due to negligence, vehicle failure, or otherwise. If at any time a participant does not accept these risks, the participant agrees not to participate in drag racing."

A safe race car is much easier to handle and maintain. It makes your racing experience more enjoyable. The following pages help you decide what modifications are needed to make your car as completive as you feel you need, but the importance of safety is your sole responsibility.

SUSPENSION BASICS AND DRAG RACING DYNAMICS

This chapter explains the basic physics occurring on the starting line when you launch your car, along with why it does (or doesn't do) what it should. Your understanding of what is happening can give you an advantage over your competitor. Put this advantage to full use, and your car will maximize its starting-line bite. Maximum bite means quicker and more consistent reaction times, as well as quicker and more consistent elapsed times (ETs).

For Every Action There is a Reaction

Let's discuss the car's physical movements while going from standing still (at an idle) to accelerating at wide-open throttle (WOT). Whatever make of car you have, the same principles apply. To further explain this discussion, the photo on this page represents a typical car making lots of torque without proper suspension modifications.

Notice the way the car lifts the driver-side front tire, and leaves the passenger side front tire on the ground. This blatant body twist affects the rear tires as well. The body roll will transfer more weight to the passenger-side rear tire, planting it harder than the driver's-side rear tire. This gives the car less-than-maximum traction while not launching straight.

The typical car drives itself to the right. Many drivers are so accustomed to this happening, they don't even realize how it affects the car. If your car leaves the starting line like the car on this page and you feel the car is leaving straight, you're wrong. Have a friend or crew member with a telephoto camera zoom in on your hand on the steering wheel while you launch. You then see how much steering correction you must add to launch the car straight. Because it's a natural reaction for a driver to correct

This Chevelle shows what a high-HP GM A-Body car can do at the starting line without the necessary modification. An anti-roll bar would greatly improve this car's launch.

the wheel, and because the car probably evolved to this point over time with gradual gains in power, correcting the wheel has become part of the launch ritual. You probably don't even realize it's happening.

Why does this twisting happen to a car that is perfectly level at the starting line? The answer is physics. For every action, there is an equal and opposite reaction. Imagine you are standing at the front of the car, looking back. I will start at the front of the car and work toward the rear, explaining how each movement is an action, followed by a reaction.

Remember to picture yourself standing at the front of the car, looking to the rear. Most novice racers

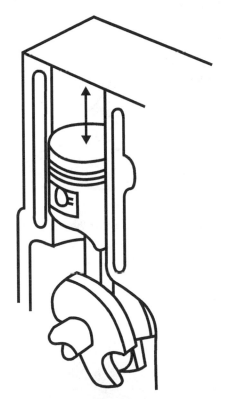

When the spark plug ignites the fuel/air mixture in the combustion chamber there is an equal force on the piston to go down as well as an equal amount of force trying to lift the engine block. But it can't because it is bolted into the car.

assume that the car in the photo on page 8 has so much horsepower, the engine is lifting the front driver's side of the car, transferring weight, and forcing the rear passenger side of the car to squat. What is really happening is much different! Let's clear up that misconception.

First of all, torque (not horsepower) makes the car accelerate from a dead stop at a fast rate of speed. Horsepower comes into effect after the car is well on its way and higher in the RPM range. Second, the car is not rolling counter-clockwise because the engine is pulling it in that direction, but rather because of a reaction.

The spark plug ignites the compressed fuel and air in the combustion chamber, driving the piston down. This rotates the crankshaft clockwise. That is the action. The illustration on this page shows the action of the exploding charge in the combustion chamber, which is driving the piston down and forcing the crankshaft clockwise while at the same time creating an equal force on the cylinder head and block trying to rotate the engine in an opposite (counter-clockwise) direction. That is the reaction. Being attached to the frame rails, the counter-clockwise rotation of the block is trying to rotate the car along with it. The more torque being generated, the greater both the action and reaction are. The more reaction there is in the chassis, the less action there is on the piston. Therefore, a chassis with enough preload (see Chapters 2, 3, and 4) to prevent body roll has more down force on the piston, allowing for more force on the crank, and therefore more usable power.

Since the crankshaft is rotating in a clockwise direction, the torque converter or clutch (and transmis-

sion) is also rotating in a clockwise direction. The transmission, with its different gear ratios, multiplies that torque even further.

For example, let's use a typical GM Turbo 400 automatic transmission with a first-gear reduction ratio of 2.48:1. That means the transmission's output should be 2.48 times its input from the converter or clutch. If your engine produces 700 ft-lbs of torque at the flywheel, then the transmission output should be 1,736 (700 x 2.48 = 1,736) pounds of torque in first gear, minus the parasitic loss in the transmission.

The clockwise-rotating transmission and driveshaft also rotate the rear axle's pinion gear in a clockwise direction. Once the pinion gear rotates in a clockwise direction, another action-versus-reaction is set up. Because the pinion gear is rotating clockwise, the entire rear-end housing tries to rotate counter-clockwise (when viewed from the front of the car, looking rearward). This causes the housing to push down on the passenger-side rear tire. If the rear passenger-side tire is being forced down (loaded), then the driver-side rear tire is being lifted (unloaded), and the housing is trying to lift that tire off the ground. Since the passenger-side rear tire is being forced to the ground by the rear-end housing rotation, less resistance is being offered against the weight transfer from the driver-side front corner. This seems good, as more weight transfer would appear to be the goal, but less resistance is not the best way to make use of this weight transfer. This is discussed in-depth in Chapter 4.

As the clockwise action of the pinion gear is attempting to rotate the ring gear, a second reaction is occurring as it pushes down upon

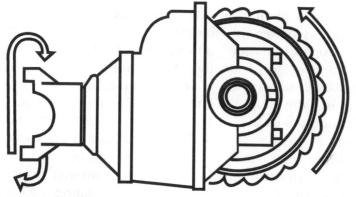

As the pinion gear turns, the pinion teeth mesh with the ring gear teeth and turn the ring gear, which then turns the axles.

the ring gear. Since the ring gear is bolted solidly into the housing (at the bearing mounts), this action now causes the rear-end housing to try to rotate clockwise. The action of the pinion turning clockwise creates two opposing reactions, and this causes wheel hop (the rear tires jumping up and down). Without enough resistance to weight transfer, the housing goes in one direction until it pushes that tire down as hard as it can. Then it rebounds and the other reaction takes over and forces the housing into the other direction. This continues as one reaction wins, and then the other, over and over again.

The illustration above shows that the pinion gear rotates the ring gear, axles, and tires in a direction that either spins the tires in a forward motion, or if the tires hook, moves the car in a forward direction. That is the action. The illustration at right (top) is the reaction—the rear-end housing is trying to rotate in the opposite direction, attempting to roll the pinion upward and the rear-end housing out of the car. This can't happen since the rear-end housing is bolted into the car's chassis. But, what does happen is that the rear-end housing and its mounts (including the control arms, ladder bars, or leaf springs) rotate on an arch (pivoting on the front leaf-spring mounts, the front ladder-bar mounts, or

the imaginary intersection of the extended upper and lower control arms) based upon the type of suspension system. The pivot point of the arch can be modified to achieve maximum traction (see Chapters 2, 3, and 4).

With the tires moving forward (without any wheel hop) and the

passenger-side rear tire being loaded along with the driver-side rear tire being unloaded, why doesn't the passenger tire push the car to the left instead of to the right as it does? This is due to tire circumference, as shown in the bottom illustration on this page. The passenger-side rear tire being loaded (forced down) becomes shorter. Since both tires are being forced to roll in a forward direction at the same rate of speed, this allows the taller side tire (with more circumference) to push the car to the right. This justifies the need for chassis preload (tricking the car to plant both rear tires equally) to move the car forward in a straight line without intervention by the driver. The right amount of chassis preload should

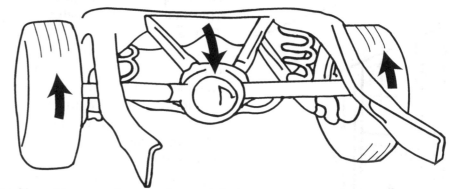

As with a piston, creating equal up and down pressure, the action of the pinion gear turning the axles, wheels, and tires in a forward direction create a reaction with the rear-end housing trying to roll the pinion up and the rear end out of the car.

Rear View of Car

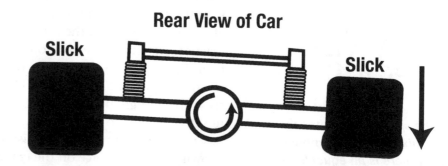

Shown from the back of the car the action of turning the pinion gear clockwise (as viewed from the front of the car) creates a reaction with the housing trying to turn counterclockwise (as viewed from the front of the car) and loading the two tires differently. Thus the need for preload in the car's suspension.

cause the car to plant both rear tires identically, creating equal tire circumference on both sides and causing the car to launch straight. For a good wheels-up launch you need the rear tires to be driving the car in as straight a line as possible.

The quickest way from point A to point B is the straightest line possible. The illustration (below left) gives a summary of this chapter. Be sure you understand it completely before you proceed.

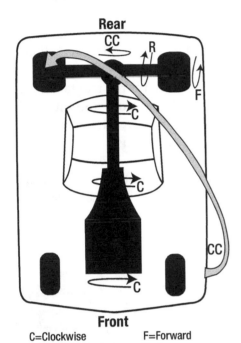

Rear

C=Clockwise F=Forward
CC=Counterclockwise R=Reverse

This drawing summarizes the discussion that for every action there is a reaction. With the engine turning the transmission and pinion gear clockwise the rear axle housing is trying to turn counterclockwise. Also, with the engine firing and igniting the gas/air mixture, the piston is being forced down and the block is being pushed up. With the block connected to the frame the entire body twists, lifting the driver-side tire 6 to 12 inches higher than the passenger-side front tire.

Shock Absorbers

One thing that is very important, yet often overlooked, are the rear shock absorbers. Even if you have the right spring on your car, it is up to the shock to control that spring. As with most race car parts, you get what you pay for. An inexpensive set of shocks (such as the ones advertised as 50/50 or a three-way adjustable) should work on cars with as much as 300 to 350 hp. However, I have seen these shocks tested on a dedicated shock dyno and very seldom are they identical to one another out of the box. Cars at this horsepower level simply don't need a lot of suspension work to make the tires hook, so even the most rudimentary upgrade shock absorbers should work. Once your car's horsepower level starts going beyond 350, I strongly suggest moving up in the quality of the shocks.

I've found that the QA1 single-adjustable (one knob) rear shocks are the next logical step up, and are good for cars with 350 to 500 hp.

QA1 single-adjustable shocks have one knob at the bottom with 18 different adjustment settings. Turning the knob counterclockwise creates a softer shock setting, while turning the knob clockwise stiffens it. There are 18 positions (or clicks) that change both the compression and extension (rebound) settings. As a car approaches 500 hp (and definitely by 600 hp), I suggest going to the QA1 double-adjustable (two knob) rear shocks, which boast 18 positions on each knob. This gives you a total of 324 different valving combinations and most importantly the ability to adjust the shock's compression independently from its extension (rebound).

Inexpensive three-way adjustable drag shock.

QA1 single adjustable shock. One knob will adjust compression at the same time.

With most adjustable shocks, it's best to start near the center of however many adjustments that particular shock has. If the front of your car needs more weight transfer (pitch rotation), a softer setting may be needed. Don't get too soft or you may lose the control your shock has on your suspension, thus allowing it to do unexpected things.

For a car that squats in the rear upon acceleration you may need to loosen the shock to get maximum weight transfer (pitch rotation). For a car that raises in the rear upon acceleration, you need to be in that middle range and careful not to get so stiff upon compression that the rear suspension does not allow the front suspension to raise.

The QA1 double adjustable shock has separate knobs to adjust compression and extension separately.

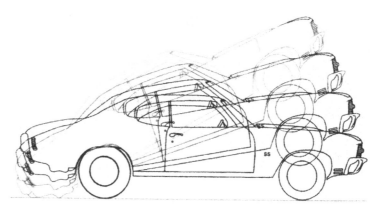

An excessive wheel stand creates rearward motion (pitch rotation) making the tires hook harder but because of this rearward motion it also makes the car harder to push forward.

Remember, if a car is standing on its back bumper, it may be getting maximum traction off the line but it's not necessarily getting maximum forward motion. Since the car is pivoting on the rear tires, the front of the car is actually going rearward in order to get to that height and making the car much harder to push forward.

Coil-Over Conversions

Due to the popularity of muscle cars, coil-over conversion kits have been developed for the rear. You can't mount a true coil-over spring and shock in the factory shock mount locations, as they were never designed to hold up the weight of the car. You can buy kits that include additional strengthening upper and lower mounts to allow these mounts to properly support the weight of the car. Also included are the coil-over shocks and matching springs, and Torrington bearings for the springs to sit upon, which make spring adjustments easier.

I have designed three kits. One raises the rear of the car 2 inches; another lowers the car 2 inches, and a third maintains the rear factory ride height. The bottom mount is also further adjustable. I have worked on muscle cars enough over the years to be able to pick the right parts for an application although you should have the rear of your car weighed to be accurate.

Once installed, the coil-over rear shock conversion controls ride height, compression, and rebound. Any or all of these can be easily adjusted and used to tune the car's launch and ride characteristics for optimal performance on the street and at the strip.

Coil-over shocks support the weight of the entire car. Factory shock mounts were never engineered to support that kind of weight, so the frame around the shock mounts must be strengthened. This kit does just that.

Proper Shock Length is Critical

With race cars no longer having stock suspension and/or different tire diameters than they shipped with, or even different tire diameters front to rear, it is very important to look at proper shock ride height. The last thing you need in any suspension is to have the shock bottom-out in either direction. When that happens, any suspension motion (pitch rotation) up to that point can dramatically stop and reverse in direction. If this happens, the rear tires (which were loaded) unload just like a rubber band is stretched, then released. The very least that can happen is you do not have maximum pitch rotation available as if you had the right shocks.

How to Measure Shock Length

If you are using conventional springs (non coil-over), everything must be installed in the car, including the driver (or something of similar weight) in the driver's seat. Here is the procedure:

1. With the car sitting on all four tires, measure the shock length from the center of the top mounting mechanism to the center of the bottom fastening mechanism whether it be a cross-bar, bushing, stud, or post.
2. Take the same measurements with the shock unmounted at one end and completely compressed.
3. Reattach the shock and put jackstands under the frame.
4. Let the rear axle come down as far as it goes and take the same measurements again.
5. Remove both rear shocks and pull them all the way down.
6. Let the floor jack down enough to see how much travel the rear end still has left. You don't want less than 1/2 inch or the shock could bottom-out. If you have excess shock travel left, you need a shock with less travel.

Manufacturers such as QA1 publish charts that allow you to find the shock that has the right travel length to match your measurements. That way there is as much travel available on compression as there is on extension (rebound), while giving you the correct ride height.

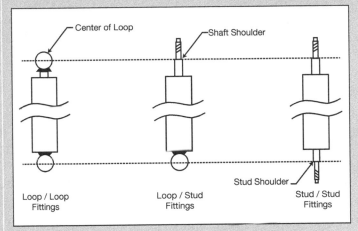

Ride height measurement must be taken from mounting point to mounting point with the car sitting on all four tires.

QA1 Shock Lengths

Compressed Height	Extended Height	Upper Mount	Lower Mount
10.13	14	Eylet	Eylet
8.75	13.5	Stud	T-Bar
10.39	15.35	Stud	Special
9.38	14.38	Stud	T-Bar
12.25	19	Stud	Eylet
13.5	21	T-Bar	Eylet
14.87	23.87	Eylet	Eylet
14.5	23.5	Stud	Eylet
15.5	24.12	Stud	Eylet

REAR SUSPENSION: LEAF SPRINGS

Rear-wheel-drive cars with leaf springs have the same issues as their coil-sprung competitors. They must have a means to set pinion angle, preload, and get the car to launch as fast as possible. In addition, a leaf-sprung car has to deal with the issue of spring wrap-up.

First I discuss some of the more popular "old school" methods. Many racers successfully still use these same methods today in bracket racing with cars probably having around 350 hp or less. Later in the chapter I discuss some of the more technologically up-to-date methods for launching rear-wheel-drive cars with leaf springs.

Pinion Angle

Pinion angle is measured in reference to the angle of the pinion gear compared to the driveshaft. As I said, *to the driveshaft*—not to the ground, transmission, engine, or any of the many other methods I have heard of. Those measurements are important for other reasons, but they have nothing to do with pinion angle. Before you go out and add to the pinion angle under your car, know that pinion angle robs horsepower as the engine overcomes the pinion angle. By "overcome," I mean the rotation of the driveshaft and pinion gear

attempt to straighten out the pinion angle and force however much pinion angle there is to zero degrees or flat. This happens no matter how much pinion angle is installed into the car. The more pinion angle there is, the more horsepower is needed (or robbed from the engine), which could be otherwise used to accelerate the car faster. This straightening process (flattening the "V" and removing the pinion angle to zero) creates a leverage affect at the front of the driveshaft and at the rear end. This leverage effect uses the weight of the car to drive the tires harder into the pavement.

Always run the least amount of pinion angle necessary to get your car to hook, but not so much as to waste horsepower. I suggest a starting point of 2 degrees negative pinion angle for cars in the 400 hp range, and maybe 4 degrees for cars in the 600 hp range. I've seen up to 7 degrees for cars running a large shot of nitrous—maybe in the range of 1,000 hp with combined engine and nitrous horsepower. When you measure your driveshaft angle (e.g., 1.5 degrees down) and the pinion angle (e.g., 3.5 degrees up in the opposite

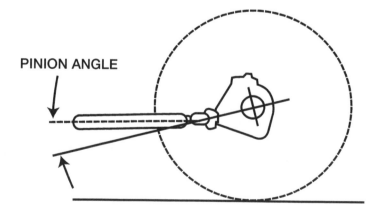

PINION ANGLE

Pinion angle represents the difference between the driveshaft and the pinion gear, nothing else. How much you choose to run can aid in tuning how your car launches.

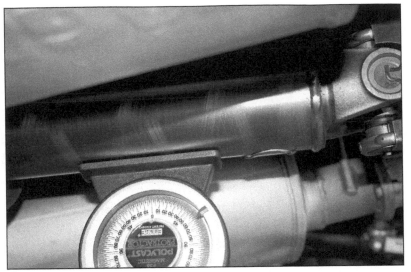

The proper technique for checking driveshaft angle is to have the vehicle at rest on a level surface with the weight on the tires. A drive-on lift is optimal. Place the angle finder on the driveshaft (as shown) and read the gauge. It's all quite simple, but many people make it more complex than it really is. Accuracy is key. Just be sure to double-check your measurements and use good-quality tools.

You need to unbolt the driveshaft and use the pinion yoke to get an accurate measurement. Again, the car has to be at rest on a level surface with the weight on the tires.

direction), adding the two together- represents 5 degrees total negative pinion angle. Make all settings with the driver or something of equal weight in the driver's seat and the car race ready. A reasonable amount of fuel should be in the tank (typically half-full). The car must be setting on all four tires inflated to race pressure. In most factory production cars, to get longevity of parts, I have seen a positive number to near zero degrees pinion angle depending upon the age of the chassis components being used, especially the springs. It is very important to get yourself an angle-measuring tool then check and correct your car's pinion angle. To change the pinion angle, wedges

can be installed between the spring mounts and the leaf springs, thus tipping the pinion either upward or downward depending upon the shim being used and its direction.

Preload and Spring Wrap

Preload and spring wrap-up can be controlled using traction bars or slapper bars, which are the most common methods used in lower-horsepower cars. A slapper bar gets its name because it bolts to the existing spring U-bolts, replacing the plate under the spring and extending forward. There are many different versions of these types of traction bars for leaf springs. A gap is left between

the snubber on the front end of the traction bar and the spring. The gap can be different on either side before slapping the frame (or the front of the spring depending upon the style in use), thus creating preload.

Moving the driver-side traction bar snubber closer to the frame creates preload, helping to keep the car from turning right. If you need more preload, adjust either the passenger-side snubber (first choice) closer to the frame or back the driver-side

This is the digital angle finder manufactured by Allstar. It's a top-notch tool and makes finding pinion angle easy and repeatable.

These leaf spring wedges are used to adjust pinion angle on vehicles equipped with rear leaf springs. The wedge is mounted between the spring mount pad and the leaf spring itself. Doing so changes the angle the axle housing sits at.

snubber (second choice) away from the frame. If your car turns right upon launch, you need more preload and should adjust the passenger-side snubber closer to the frame. If your car turns left upon launch, then you need less preload and should adjust the passenger-side snubber farther away from the frame. Remember, the more distance the snubber is from the frame (or spring) the longer it takes before the car reacts to your settings.

For those of you running rear-wheel-drive GM cars with leaf springs, Landrum Spring Company makes what they refer to as a Parabolic leaf spring. The Parabolic spring is a mono-leaf design that is thicker in the middle and tapers as it moves closer to the ends of the spring. This thinner leaf at the end allows the car to plant the rear tires quicker and harder. The thicker middle part of the spring helps prevent spring wrap-up. You still need some sort of slapper bar or a set of CalTracs traction bars to stiffen up the front half of the spring.

Chrysler muscle cars have the option of Mopar super stock springs. They have a heavier spring rate on the passenger side than on the driver side, thus creating preload. Additionally, they are much stiffer in the front half of the spring (due to the axle not being centered on the spring) than the rear half, creating a rear suspension that works like a ladder-bar setup. I have used this style of springs in a GM Oldsmobile Omega race car that I once had with a mild 455 Olds engine, and they worked great helping me win the IHRA Milan Northern Nationals.

I always liked to see the Chrysler Super Stock cars leave the starting line. You could tell how good they were, planting the rear tires, by the amount of separation visible between the leaves in the back half of the springs. Eventually, spring clamps were used to eliminate this separation and to create even better 60-foot times, as the lesser amounts of separation caused the tire to be pushed into the pavement quicker.

The Mopar super stock spring name came from the fact they were developed in the late 1960s by Chrysler for its NHRA Super Stock race cars to give them maximum traction with minimum research and an advantage over the GM and Ford Super Stock cars of the time. The Big Three car manufacturers were heavily into drag racing and lived by the motto "Win on Sunday, sell on Monday" in the hope that customers see a car win a race on Sunday and want to buy one on Monday.

Some of the more notable Chrysler Super Stock racers were the Mancini brothers, who produced a string of successful Chrysler factory-backed race cars. Mancini Racing used that race experience to grow into a parts business that sells suspension parts for Chrysler race cars.

Whether you are using Chrysler super stock springs or not, the ride height can be controlled by re-arching the existing leaf springs. Most large cities still have businesses that re-arch springs for truck or trailer applications, and should be able to do your car springs.

These bolt-on slapper bars from Competition Engineering are typical and affordable. They are easy to install and can be used to adjust suspension preload while stiffening the front half of the spring. Most leaf-spring-equipped street-based cars can benefit from having them, and if they can be used to help tune the suspension, that's even better.

This is my former Olds Omega drag car. I used Chrysler's proven super stock leaf springs under the rear of it with great success. The car didn't know they were Chrysler parts.

This is Dan Zrust in a 1968 Plymouth Barracuda. The car competes in the notoriously tough Super Stock ranks and is powered by the venerable 426-ci Chrysler Hemi engine. This shot was taken at the 2009 NHRA U.S. Nationals in Indianapolis, Indiana.

Here is a classic shot of legendary Mopar racer Ray Mancini from 1969. He's shown piloting a 1964 Dodge, powered by a 426 Hemi engine at the NHRA World Finals in Dallas, Texas.

Rise or Squat

Should the rear suspension rise or squat upon launch? The location of the front mount (height in the chassis) of the rear-end leaf spring determines whether the car lifts in the rear or squats in the rear when leaving the starting line. If the mount is above the neutral line, the chassis lifts in the rear. If the mount is below the neutral line, the chassis squats in the rear.

I have tried to drive the point home that a car which lifts in the rear will plant the rear tires harder. This is true to a point. I am assuming the average reader of this book will not be driving/building a 7-second quarter-mile car the first time out. You first must understand the basics.

However, there is a point in horsepower-to-weight ratio that some cars with higher horsepower levels (800 to 1,000) need the front of the leaf spring mount to be lowered. Thirty years ago most full-bodied cars benefitted from a higher front leaf spring mount. With today's horsepower the mount needs to be much lower. Using the drawing on page 18 the fact of whether the car lifts or squats in the rear depends upon where the front spring mount is in relation to the neutral line.

Lower-horsepower cars can use a higher mount thus making the car lift in the rear upon launch. As horsepower levels (800 to 1,000) increase, the mount needs to be lowered. The reason for the necessary lower mount is high-speed stability. A car lifting in the rear plants the tires harder but with that same lift at the top end it loses traction. With today's tires lower-horsepower cars have sufficient traction. Now as the horsepower gets higher and higher (more than 1,000) the car has the ability to break the tires loose on the top end. For safety and to be able to complete the run the front spring mount needs to be lowered.

However the opposite occurs at the starting line. Most 1,000-plus-hp cars today have some sort of power adder (NOS, blower, supercharger) and can adjust the starting line power to compensate.

Every car/chassis is different. There is no exact measurement.

What works just right for one car won't necessarily be right for another car. The idea here is to experiment. As long as you have the knowledge, you can make it work—through trial and error.

Put that same no-hop bar on a Mustang (also a factory 4-link suspension) with the same horsepower-to-weight ratio and it will hook for about 6 inches and then blow the tires off. The Mustang has the engine much closer to the rear end than the GM intermediate thus giving the rear control arms a completely different leverage affect. Today's 7-second quarter-mile ET nitrous oxide cars running on a 10.5-inch tire will not use a no-hop bar. In fact they will either raise the rear of the lower control arm or if permitted lower the front of the lower control arm to almost level and leave the upper control arm in its factory location (different class rules allow different modifications).

For high-speed acceleration, the intersection point needs to be much further out in the car for top-end stability. A car that lifts in the rear will hit the rear tire harder. You can hit the rear tire too hard and go into tire spin or tire shake. There sometimes needs to be a compromise. Less hit at the starting line (where power can be brought in slowly) for more traction at the far end (so the car can develop more miles per hour and still go straight).

With today's tires a car running in the low 10-second ET in the quarter-mile which lifts in the rear after the front end has lifted (pitch rotation) can use the harder hit off the line successfully. As the car gets further out and the chassis settles down, today's tires still provide enough traction for the car to stay hooked and drive straight all the way to the finish line. Keep in mind that if a car is lifting in the rear and the front is not lifting, the car is actually transferring weight to the front (reverse pitch rotation) and removing weight from the rear tires and having less possible traction.

Now look at a 7-second NOS quarter-mile ET car with more than 1,800 hp. The front mount needs to be even lower for top end traction, which causes a loss of traction at the starting line. Timers add the nitrous in stages with each stage farther down track. There is only one stage or no nitrous at the starting line.

Since the car does not have a lower front spring mount it will have better leverage down track and will not be trying to lift in the rear down track and therefore have more weight pushing on the rear tires providing better traction during the 175+ mph runs.

Just as 1,000 hp is an arbitrary point at which a car can turn left instead of turning right at the starting launch, it can also be used as an arbitrary point that a car needs the front leaf spring mount much lower in the chassis.

The Neutral Line

The neutral line is a reference point used when considering weight transfer (pitch rotation) in suspended cars. It begins at a point above the front spindle centerline as high off the ground as the center of gravity of your car, and continues to the rear tire contact patch directly below the rear axle centerline. If the front mount of the rear-end leaf spring is above the neutral line, the rear of the car raises upon launch. Chapters 3 and 4 explain how to get the pivot point farther rearward in the car. The opposite is true with most rear-wheel-drive cars with leaf springs if the car is making a lot of horsepower, as they already have a pivot point too far rearward. The closer the front mount of the rear-end leaf spring is to the rear axle, the harder the suspension hits the rear tires (of course, you can overpower a tire). If this same front mount of the rear-end leaf spring is below the neutral line, the car squats upon launch.

A car that lifts in the rear pushes down harder on the rear tires. You can't lift 100 pounds without putting 100 pounds of extra pressure on your feet. However, moving the front mount of the rear-end leaf spring too close to the rear end causes the car to hit the tire too hard. It's possible to overpower a tire causing it to wrap up like a rubber band. When it can't wrap any more, it unwraps (like a

The adjustable pinion snubber limits how far the rear axle housing is allowed to rotate. These are popular with Chrysler racers and this one is available from the Mopar experts at Mancini Racing.

spring), allowing the tire to unload and lose traction. Too hard of a hit on the tires may work some of the time at some tracks but not all of the time at all tracks.

For the Chrysler cars, Mancini Racing is now offering an adjustable pinion snubber. This unit fits to the center front of the rear axle housing. It helps control axle wind-up by adjusting the height of this snubber to the floorpan, depending on the individual requirement. This provides a more precise adjustment and locking than any other snubber on the market today. Snubber height is obtained by turning the threaded shaft up or down. When the bumper is at the desired height, it is locked in place by screwing the lock nut down tightly onto the tube top. This unit is CNC-machined to ensure manufacturing consistency and quality throughout.

If you could lift a car off the ground at its center of gravity the car would not roll in any direction—neither sideways nor front to rear. Center of gravity calculation is a very complicated and mathematical procedure. Solid spacers must replace the shocks. Two 10-inch-tall blocks and a set of scales are also needed. First weigh the front of the car, then lift the rear of the car 10 inches by setting the scales on the 10-inch blocks and reweigh the front of the car. Then plug all of this information into a mathematical formula. Instead, use the camshaft centerline as the center of gravity when figuring the neutral line.

While not as accurate, it serves to use in calculating the neutral line for reference to see if the car will rise or squat. Having the exact center of gravity is not important, understanding the principals involved in this discussion is. No two cars respond

the same with the same settings. One front leaf spring mounting point that works the best in a certain car may be completely wrong for a another car. Do your homework and determine what is best for your car.

Ladder Bars

Ladder bars are a great asset to making a rear-wheel-drive car with leaf springs work. This is because they relocate the pivot point farther forward in the car by having a lower mounting point than the front mount of the rear-end leaf spring, therefore making the mounting point closer to the neutral line. By having a lower pivot point, the car isn't as violent and doesn't overpower the rear slicks. You can also lower the pivot point by lowering the front of the spring mount hole in the frame. If you have class rules not allowing this modification, an old trick is to weld the old hole shut, grind it off flush so it doesn't show, and relocate the hole lower.

Subframe Connectors

Most rear-wheel-driven cars with leaf springs are unibody designs with subframes. This means they don't have a full ladder-type frame from the front of the car to the rear. Instead, the frame and body are assembled as a single unit. The front subframe (engine bay) is connected to the floorpan as is the rear subframe (rear suspension area). Structural integrity is designed into the vehicle's integral body/floorpan/stub chassis assembly.

These unibody designs proved to be adequate for production car use and cost less to mass produce. They

This Advanced Chassis ladder-bar setup has double adjusters for setting pinion angle and suspension preload. Ladder-bar setups are great on the drag strip, but not so great on the street. They tie the control arms together, which is fine for straight-line acceleration but detrimental to cornering.

typically result in a lighter-weight car, so fuel economy concerns were addressed as well. Under race conditions, unibody cars tend to flex a lot more since they don't have the full-frame chassis to prevent twist

These subframe connectors are typical for a unibody car and were designed for use under a Chrysler product. Subframe connectors tie the front and rear of the car together to make it stronger and less likely to flex. They are equally popular with drag enthusiasts and corner carvers.

under heavy loading. To correct this, subframe connectors that connect the front subframe rails with the rear subframe rails should be installed. This greatly stiffens the car and helps reduce body twist, making the car respond better to hard-launch conditions.

These handy prefabricated connector packages let you tie the front and rear subframe longitudinally. Most frame connectors can be bolted or welded in, depending on individual preference and the design of the connector. When installing your roll bar or roll cage, be sure to tie the front subframe, rear subframe, and subframe connectors all together.

Calvert Leaves

Having spent most of my years drag racing in muscle cars with coil springs, I decided to contact John Calvert (from Calvert Racing Suspensions) to get some ideas on the latest technology in making rear-wheel-drive cars with leaf-spring rear suspensions hook, even though the same old issues still exist of setting pinion angle, preload, getting the car to launch as fast as possible, and controlling spring wrap-up. Here is a summary of what John had to say when I asked him about how to get a leaf-sprung car to hook:

"The short answer is, 'With a balanced approach and a lot of testing.' Several areas can contribute to the success of quick, efficient, and consistent 60-foot times. Some of the areas have a great deal to do with success and some hardly affect it at all. Many cars are sensitive to certain settings or components and not so worried about others."

Weight

"We [Calvert Racing Suspensions] deal with a wide variety of drag cars. We might see a car that weighs around 3,300 pounds, runs a big-block engine that puts out 500 to 600 hp, has a 3-speed automatic transmission, uses a transmission brake, has a pair of 29x10-inch slicks, and runs 10-second ETs in the quarter-mile. We may see a 1,200- to 1,500-hp car running nitrous oxide, a 2-speed automatic transmission, running on drag radial tires, deep into the 7-second range in the quarter-mile. Even trucks, small ones, full-sized, and Diesels.

"We offer a suspension package for these vehicles that was developed over the years, first with the introduction of our now-famous CalTrac traction bars, then a unique split mono-leaf spring, an adjustable rear shock, and finishing the package with a 90/10 front shock. It seemed each step brought out a new obstacle to address."

Center of Gravity

"In the beginning there was a trash can. Yes, I remember reading an article which explained how pushing a car was like pushing a refrigerator or kicking a trash can. This was (and still is) a very important thought. So, go ahead, kick away and see where you have to kick to get that can to slide right across the floor. Now how do you kick a car?

"First, lift it like an airplane. Hold it like you would to find the center of gravity (CG). It's normally nose heavy, so maybe around where the steering wheel is, draw a plane (not an airplane) to divide the car in half with the line. Now put the car on a rotisserie and find out where the points need to be in order to spin it to be balanced. Draw another line

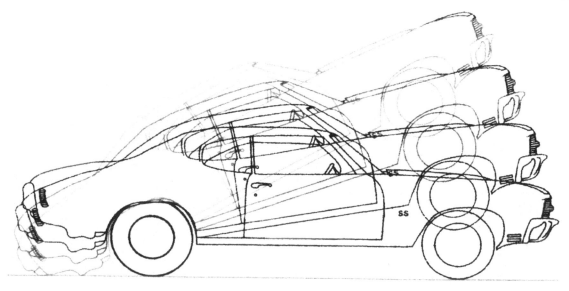

An excessive wheelstand creates rearward motion, which is not the way we're trying to go. Upward motion is good, but rearward motion can be counterproductive. Lifting the front end a few inches is just about as good as it gets.

through the car. Where the line intersects through the plane is the point it needs to be balanced. Now push with a vector that starts at the rear tire patch and aims through the front attaching point of your leaf spring (the spring eye) and see where it goes.

"If it's a normal leaf-spring car, it goes too far back. If it's a traditional Mopar with 20-inch front half-leaf springs, it goes way too far back (too much down pressure on those tires). This is why ladder bars were developed—to move the attaching point forward and correct the pushing vector.

"An NRHA rule for Stock Eliminator cars states: 'No part of the traction system can extend forward of the front spring eye, and it has to be a bolt-on device.' Lower the attaching point. Now the pushing point has been corrected and you can really put the power to the car, pushing the car with the tire. With the CalTrac traction system we are controlling leaf-spring wrap-up (this is mandatory) and correcting the pushing point (or at least making it better), and giving some other benefits like side-to-side preload and total preload on the rear springs. This gives some adjustability to the rear suspension. I love adjustability. I know no two cars are alike even if they are alike. The pushing point and adjustability in the back is very important.

"Leaf-spring suspensions are like all others in drag racing in that they need a coefficient of friction between the tire and track surface to allow the suspension to be a player. There are a large number of considerations when discussing leaf-spring cars. Whether the car's purpose is to work well on the street, street and strip, or strictly on the strip, the more drag race you want, the less street you get. The instant center of a leaf-sprung vehicle is typically too far back, resulting in excessive down pressure on the tires and a requirement to employ methods to control it. This is how we do it."

Shock Absorbers

"Rear shock absorbers are one of the main items to consider. Control of the rear end is paramount to successful launches. Shock absorbers control the separation in the back. Typically,

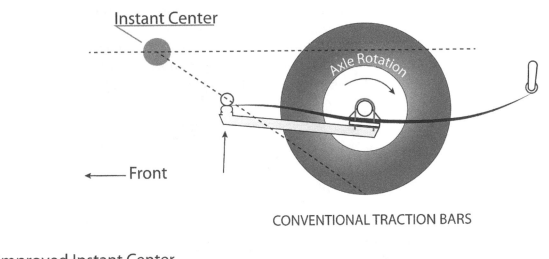

CONVENTIONAL TRACTION BARS

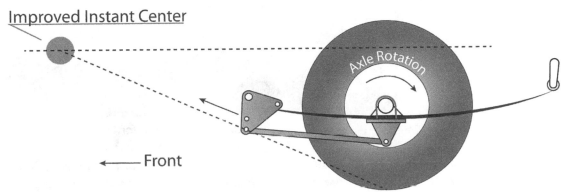

CalTracs bars versus slapper bars. Notice the better instant center location (being moved forward) due to the lower mounting point of the CalTracs bar when compared to a traditional slapper bar. CalTracs bars cost more, but they do more, so it's justified. It's no surprise CalTracs bars are very popular in all the classes where they are legal upgrades.

The light is green and the Mustang is off. Note the differences compared to the photo below left—both the front and rear suspensions are raising. The nose comes up due to rotation, and the rear of the car comes up as the suspension works to push down on the rear tires. The wheelie bar is planted, limiting the car from rotating rearward. You can bet this car is fast since it's using all of its power to plant the rear tires equally and move forward.

the rear is always trying to separate so an adjustable rear shock is essential. No control in the back of a leaf-sprung car results in great initial traction, but terrible secondary traction.

"A certain amount of violence can also be diminished with a good set of rear shocks. Good-quality shocks on the back are needed. That doesn't mean they have to be expensive. They just need to be adjustable for rate of separation. The forces trying to push the rear tire down on a leaf-sprung car are tremendous. Cheap little shocks don't do unless your car runs in the 15-second range, and then your car doesn't need anything. But as the car gains in power and you improve in its ability to get a hold of the track (slicks), you need better things.

"Rear shocks come right after traction bars. Now you can start controlling the rear end and how much down pressure you want it to have. Or, if you are observant, how much down pressure the car can handle. Keep in mind the down pressure theorem: 'You can only give as much down pressure to the rear end as the front end will react to.'"

Leaf Springs

"Leaf springs fit right in to the 'as the power increases' need. As more power is developed, a higher spring rate is needed to control it, and the platform needs to be reinforced so aftermarket springs become important. Every conceivable combination has been used/tried over time—mono-leaf, multi-leaf, a stack of leaves on the front and only one out the back and then incorporate coil-over shocks, thick multi-leaf, add a leaf to the multi stack, and finally the split-mono design.

A bit too much rotation and you're on the back bumper. Not only is energy being used to push this car rearward on this particular launch, but how aerodynamic do you figure this is? A slight adjustment is all it takes to make this better, and since this was during time trials it was the right time to experiment.

This new Cobra Jet is only moving forward. The front tires are tippy-toeing on the pavement, with just enough raise in the front end to load the rear tires heavily. The rear slicks are biting for all they're worth. This is a great launch with no wasted momentum.

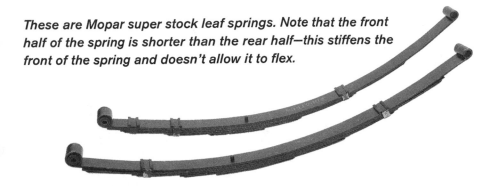

These are Mopar super stock leaf springs. Note that the front half of the spring is shorter than the rear half—this stiffens the front of the spring and doesn't allow it to flex.

"The split-mono design because it's lightweight and it emulates the parabolic mono-leaf, but allows a certain amount of adjustability. By overlapping the front half to the back half it can be used at different thicknesses front and rear, change the arch on the back to accommodate ride height, and experiment with a number of combinations looking for that perfect spring for each application.

"Control of leaf-spring wrap-up used to be the job of the traction bars. Redirecting the pushing point of the car is now accomplished through the connection point and preload adjustments on our systems. Additional power is controlled and used more efficiently. In 2010, Al Jiminez became the first leaf-sprung car driver to make a 200-mph pass in the quarter-mile. One of the advantages of the four-link and ladder bar suspensions used to be

their ability to change the instant center (pushing point) of the car. A bolt-on traction system for leaf-spring cars can now make that correction.

"A note here on spring perches. A universal perch allows you to sandwich the leaf spring between the perch and the shock mount. If you would like to experiment with a change in pinion angle, just loosen the U-bolts and slide in a wedge. The main problem with the GM-style perch is that they were designed to be used with a rubber insulator and they lack a method of interfacing the leaf-spring center pins to the perch. Additionally, to remove the insulator, spacer plates are needed to allow the spring to be properly clamped. In order to use the universal style you need to reinforce the back side to keep it from bending. We designed a perch that incorporates a better interface (more contact area) with

the axle tube and it has built-in reinforcing tabs. We market it as a heavy-duty perch.

"The bigger the tire, the better the bite. Most leaf-spring-equipped cars rarely get the luxury of bigger tires. Normally, the need to make way for the tire means the springs get moved inboard. Since there is a lot of fabrication going on, a four-link or ladder-bar set up is installed with coil-over springs."

Starting-Line RPM

"One of the areas of experimentation when dialing in a suspension is the starting-line engine speed (RPM). Be conservative in the beginning to analyze what is going on in the rest of the suspension, and then slowly adjust to find the most the car will take and still be successful. If you are foot-braking the car, you are limited to leaving the starting-line RPM to no more than the RPM just before the car's suspension starts to react. Otherwise you will use up part of the cars suspension travel before ever launching the car and not leaving as much as you could have for the launch."

Coefficient of Friction

Coefficient of friction between the track and tire depends on tire pressure that is at least close to where

This 1968 Charger got a good bite at the initial hit of the throttle—enough to pull the front tires off the ground. However, it then went into tire spin. Time for some tuning. This pass won't be optimal, and it'll show up on his time slip from the 60-foot time to the final quarter-mile elapsed time.

This early Fairlane has a solid bite on the track. The front wheels are up a bit, and the slick is being pushed down and loaded up. You know this was a good pass.

it needs to be, and that usually means to the 1/4 pound. Normally on a lightweight, tube-chassis-equipped car with wide tires, that would be about 6 pounds. On a foot-brake, full-bodied car, tire pressure could be around 12 pounds, and adding drag radials it will go up to around 18 pounds.

Although John and I explain the same thing in different ways, the end results are the same: to give you enough information about rear-wheel-drive cars with leaf springs so you can put it to use and make your car hook the way it should for your application.

This Nova's back tires are moving, but the front ones are not. That means tire spin. Unless you're in the burnout box, that's bad news.

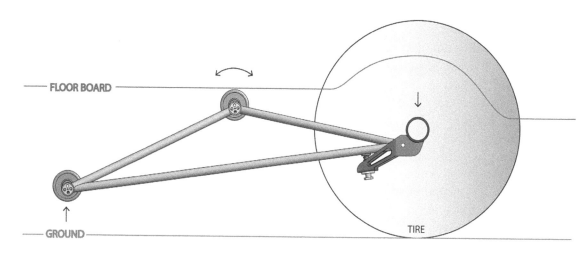

You thought all a wheelie bar could do was stop the car from flipping over backward, but the smart guys at Calvert Racing figured out how to harness this energy and use it to push down harder on the tires. Innovations like this make people wonder why this wasn't thought of a long time ago.

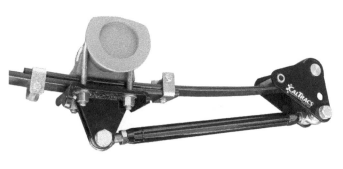

Here's another look at a CalTracs setup. There's a lot to see here if you know where to look. Notice the minimal mono-leaf setup, the heavy-duty hardware, and the simple adjustments that can be made without removing the arm from the car. The length of the arm can be changed by loosening the jambnuts and twisting the arm. Nice and easy.

This is the split mono-leaf spring setup. It's a lot lighter than the factory spring stack it replaces, and less likely to wrap up as well. Many different spring ratings can be had to suit the needs of just about any car or truck.

REAR SUSPENSION: COIL SPRINGS AND THREE-LINK

This chapter looks at muscle cars with rear-suspension systems using coil springs with two lower control arms and a torque tube. These factory three-link cars include GM 1982 to 2002 Camaros and Firebirds (also referred to as third- and fourth-generation F-Body cars). Since rear-wheel-drive cars with rear coil springs, two lower control arms, and a torque tube did not have upper and lower control arms with opposing angles like the factory four-link cars, it was also necessary to add a track locater (called a Panhard bar).

General Motors promoted Firebirds and Camaros as performance cars, and the design engineers at General Motors developed a much better suspension system than the earlier factory four-link. This three-link system worked well for drag racing applications with minor modifications.

The Neutral Line

Extending an imaginary line forward on the same angle as the lower control arms, it crosses the torque tube that is attached to a bracket mounted to the rear-end housing. The front of the torque tube is attached to the tailshaft housing of the transmission. This intersection point determines whether the car lifts or squats in the rear when leaving the line as compared to the neutral line.

The neutral line is a reference point used when considering weight transfer (pitch rotation) in suspended cars. It begins at a point above the front spindle centerline as high off the ground as the center of gravity and continues to the rear tire contact-patch directly below the rear-axle centerline. If the intersection point of the control arms and torque tube is above the neutral line, the rear of the car raises upon

Amy Faulk flies down the track in her fourth-gen Trans-Am. This car runs strong, producing stellar 1.31-second 60-foot times, covering the eighth-mile in 6.557 seconds at 101.48 mph, and running the full quarter-mile in 10.443 seconds at 126.89 mph, consistently.

launch. The closer the intersection point is to the rear-end housing, the harder the suspension hits the rear tires (just remember you can over-power the tires). If this same intersection point is below the neutral line, the car squats upon launch.

A car that lifts in the rear has to push down harder on the tire to do so, just as you can't lift 100 pounds of something without putting 100 pounds of extra pressure on your feet. The Camaros and Firebirds already had an imaginary intersection point above the neutral line from the factory, so with no modification these cars planted the tire hard and without any wheel hop. That fact, along with the car having a short wheelbase (101 inches, compared to a Chevelle's 112 inches) made these cars an excellent candidate for doing huge wheel stands.

Several modifications were necessary to make the rear suspension of these cars an optimal contender. Since these cars came with only 24-inch-diameter tires, running a large-diameter slick in the stock wheel well was impossible. To overcome this, it was necessary to install a 2-inch-thick aluminum spacer between the top of the spring and the frame. This lifts the body over the rear end enough to allow the installation of a 9x30-inch slick. Once the rear end is lifted with the spring spacers, the Panhard bar (being fixed in length) pulls the rear axle to one side and the wheels are no longer centered (side-to-side) in the wheel-well openings. It is now necessary to install an adjustable Panhard bar. I have TIG-welded chrome-moly (for light weight and more strength) Panhard bars in a fixed length for factory ride-height cars and an adjustable Panhard bar for cars that use a non-factory ride height.

This is an exploded view of the GM F-Body three-link factory suspension design. The torque arm (1) runs between the rear axle housing and the tailshaft of the transmission. Note the Panhard bar (2) located lengthwise behind the axle. This locates the rear axle under the car and prevents it from moving left or right during hard cornering.

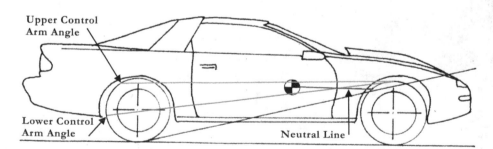

If the intersection point of the torque tube and lower control arms is above the neutral line, the car raises in the rear while launching. This plants the rear tires harder.

Preload

The suspension had no means of preload from the factory. Typically, when the tires of a Camaro or

Firebird stick, they launch the car toward the right as it leaves the line. Since these cars had no upper control arms for adjusting preload, the only thing that can be done is to install an air bag in the passenger-side rear coil-spring (or a much heavier and taller passenger-side rear coil-spring). Using an airbag is the easiest way to accomplish preload as the air bag is adjustable. Using a heavier and taller spring requires you to replace the spring every time you want to make an adjustment. Twenty-five pounds of air is usually the normal operating pressure used in an air bag in the passenger-side spring with close to 0 pounds or no air bag at all in the driver-side spring. You may need to adjust air pressure based on the car's combination. If the car still turns toward the right, add more air in the passenger-side air bag. If it turns to the left, it has too much air in the passenger-side air bag. Make changes in 2-pound increments up or down. Too big a change does not allow you to discover the best-possible pressure for your car's combination.

The best way to be aware of what is happening is to videotape your hand on the steering wheel as you launch the car. Growing up in the snowy state of Michigan, I have very good instinctive reflexes if sliding around while leaving the line. Sometimes your instinctive reactions to correct the cars launch are so natural that you don't notice them. That is why it is very important to record either hand on the steering wheel and mark the steering wheel with a white

This is a typical coil-spring spacer, to be mounted in the spring pocket below the coil. It can be a useful tool when adjusting ride height.

This is an air bag. They get installed inside coil springs, and can be inflated to varying pressures to alter the additional support they offer the spring. This air bag is manufactured by AirLift, others are similar.

Preload can also be engineered into the springs themselves. This pair of rear coil springs have different heights. The taller spring on the right is designed for the passenger's side of the car, where preload is typical under GM intermediate cars of the 1960s and 1970s when they are modified for improved drag strip performance.

A simple piece of white tape has been installed at the top/center of the steering wheel. This shows up on video, and serves to show whether the wheel is being turned (and how much, and in which direction) upon launch.

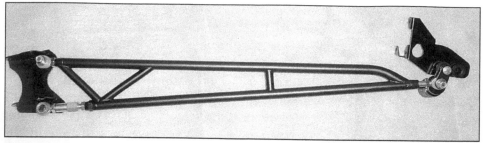

An adjustable torque tube can be used to fine-tune the launch under the GM F-Body (Camaro/Firebird) cars that came with three-link rear suspension systems. The factory arm is relatively weak and non-adjustable. This adjustable aftermarket replacement is much stronger, so it won't flex under heavy loads.

or contrasting stripe at 12 o'clock (with the front wheels straight) that shows well in the video. The video shows you if the steering wheel is turned right or left to correct a less than desirable launch. This testing can only be accurate if the car hooks at the starting line. A car with spinning tires naturally slides side-to-side or only one way just because of the spinning tires.

Pinion Angle

Factory pinion angle (which is near zero for longer U-joint life) needs to be modified. Since there were no upper arms, there's really no way to set pinion angle for a harder bite. I developed my own torque tube with a built in adjuster for the F-Body cars that allows pinion angle to be set to a more desirable setting. This torque tube is TIG-welded chrome-moly and looks similar to a long ladder bar.

To make pinion angle adjustments, the car needs to be sitting on all four tires with the driver or someone of similar weight sitting in the passenger seat. Using an angle finder, measure the driveshaft angle and then the pinion angle. Once you have the driveshaft angle, you may need to unbolt the driveshaft to get the pinion angle using the differential yoke that the driveshaft bolts up to.

Quite often there is a flat spot on each side of the rear cover where the axle tubes are pressed in on GM rear ends. This should be machined 90 degrees to the pinion. Normally the driveshaft and the pinion angles make the shape of a very flat letter "V." If so, you need to add the two angles together to get the present pinion angle.

To this point, I've said nothing about the transmission or the ground. While both have an importance while building the car, pinion angle is only the difference between the pinion and driveshaft. Nothing else! From the factory, your car probably has next to 0 degrees of pinion angle. Each car needs its own setting. Too little pinion angle and the car doesn't hook well. Too much pinion angle and the car hooks, but at a loss of horsepower. The pinion and driveshaft, no matter how much pinion angle you are using, want to straighten out under hard acceleration. That creates a leverage effect that drives the tire into the

An angle finder is an affordable tool that works wonderfully for checking pinion angle.

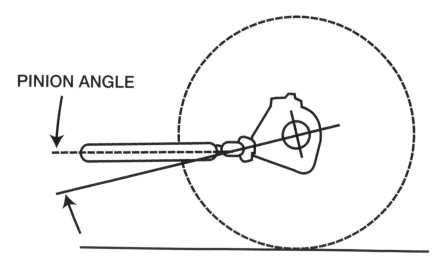

PINION ANGLE

The angle of the pinion gear is critical to how your drag car launches. Since it tries to move up, you can use this energy to help plant the rear tires. Just don't overdo it.

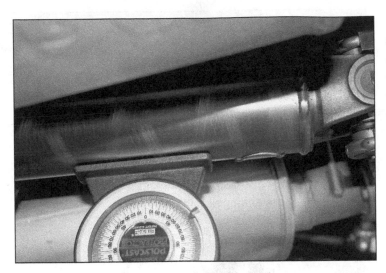

The angle finding tool is used to check driveshaft angle and pinion angle.

Here you can see the angle finder mounted on the rear of the rear axle housing. This is a good place to take the measurement on GM rear axles, as it's typically flat.

pavement. However, it robs horsepower to make this leverage effect happen. Therefore, never run more pinion angle than your car's combination requires.

As mentioned earlier, start with 2 degrees negative pinion angle for cars in the 400-hp range, 4 degrees for cars in the 600-hp range, and up to 7 degrees for cars running 1,000 hp or more. Very seldom does any car need more than 7 degrees of negative pinion angle.

When you measure your driveshaft angle (e.g., 1.5 degrees down) and the pinion angle (e.g., 3.5 degrees down in the opposite direction), adding the two together represents 5 degrees total negative pinion angle. To change the pinion angle, simply loosen the jamnuts locking the adjuster in place on the torque tube. Turn the adjuster to make the arm longer for more pinion angle or shorter for less pinion angle. Remeasure and repeat if necessary. When you have the total pinion angle you desire, lock the jamnuts in place.

Now you can see why all the top-quality adjusters are double adjustable, meaning no bolts need to be removed to make changes. Single-adjustable adjusters require one end to be removed to make changes, which makes the process more difficult and more lengthy.

Bushings

The factory soft rubber bushings in the lower control arms were another issue. Even though Camaros and Firebirds were promoted as performance cars, the design engineers had to incorporate a combination of maximum comfort, stability, and traction. Unfortunately for performance enthusiasts, stability and traction gave way to comfort. With soft rubber bushings in each end of the control arms, a quiet suspension with a soft ride was achieved. These arms are what hold the rear-end housing in the car, along with the torque tube. The front of the two lower control arms are attached to the frame rails and the rear to the rear axle housing.

To improve performance, the bushings in the lower control arms should be replaced with polyurethane bushings, such as those made by Energy Suspension. These greatly improve the handling of

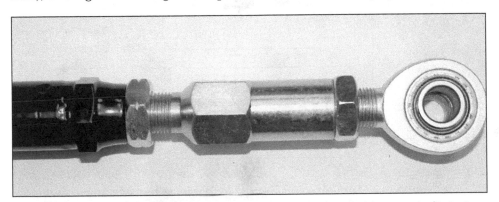

This turnbuckle-type adjuster can be adjusted without requiring any bolts to be removed from under the vehicle. The jamnuts are broken loose, and the adjuster can be lengthened or shortened by twisting it in place. The jamnuts are then tightened again to lock in the new setting. It saves a lot of time and effort.

Rear Control Arm Bushing Upgrade:

Over the years I have replaced a few rear control arm bushings and have talked to many customers who have replaced theirs. Here's a quick run-down of the easiest way to remove them:

1. Drill a complete circle of holes in the rubber bushings. This relieves the pressure from the molded rubber and allows you to eventually push out or cut out the remaining inner portion of the bushing.
2. Cut through the remaining outer rubber portion of the bushing and pry it loose from the outer steel shell.
3. If new steel outer shells are included with the bushing use a chisel to collapse and remove the remaining outer steel shell.
4. Disassemble the bushing and install the outside or the steel shell.
5. Grease the inside of the installed steel shell.

6. Next, grease the outside of the polyurethane bushing and install it into the new or existing steel shell.
7. Now grease the inside of the installed polyurethane bushing and the outside of the steel inner sleeve and insert it into the polyurethane bushing.
8. With both ends of the control arm done, grease the sides of the assembled bushing and you are ready to install the control arm back in the car.

This could be all that is necessary for cars with minimal horsepower. However, the car still has very flexible factory control arms which is not good for the consistency necessary for today's drag race cars. If your control arms are not boxed-in from the factory the next step up (which should be done before you install the new polyurethane bushings) is to box-in the control arms. Welding a steel plate to the bottom side of the control arms greatly increases the rigidity and strength of the control arm.

To remove the factory rubber control arm bushings, drill holes in a circle all the way around the bushing insert as shown. Then, push the bushing portions out, using a press. Be careful not to damage the control arm while using the press.

Depending on which bushing you're replacing, it may or may not have an outer shell. This Energy Suspension polyurethane replacement bushing does have a steel outer shell.

This is also a factory lower control arm with boxing plates added at the factory to minimize flex. These were only offered in cars with high-performance option packages like the Chevelle Super Sport (SS).

Rubber to Polyurethane

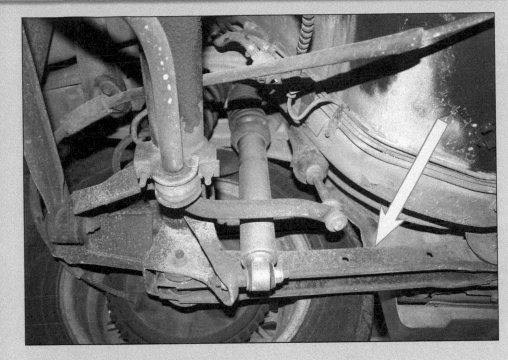

A factory-stamped steel control arm is near the bottom of this photo. These were formed from single pieces of steel into a U-shape, and they tend to flex under load.

Here are some typical polyurethane control arm bushings. These replace the factory rubber inserts and don't flex nearly as much. This set is from Energy Suspension.

This is a modern, tubular lower control arm. It is much stronger than the factory boxed arm, and comes complete with greaseable polyurethane bushings already installed. They represent the strongest design available.

Lower Control Arms

a car whether it be hard cornering or just aggressive driving. All four bushings in the lower control arms must be replaced. For ease of replacement, remove one arm at a time, complete the polyurethane bushing installation, and then reinstall that arm before moving on to the next arm.

Even with boxed lower control arms and polyurethane bushings the factory control arms are still formed from thin mild steel and not rigid enough for truly heavy-duty drag racing applications. I have developed tubular chrome-moly lower control arms with greaseable Zerk fittings for each bushing to keep them well lubricated. Chrome-moly tubing is lighter in weight and far stronger than mild steel. Chrome-moly tubing is much

lighter and less bulky than aluminum. Using chrome-moly tubing builds strength into these arms not found in other materials while still being lighter in weight than aluminum or mild steel.

The front of the torque tube is attached inside a rubber mount within a steel bracket bolted to the transmission tailshaft housing; the rear of the torque tube is bolted solid to the rear-end housing. As explained in Chapter 1, under hard launches, the rear-end housing is attempting

One Cool Tool

The digital angle finder from Allstar Performance is well worth the extra dollars in my opinion. Not only is it digital, making it much easier to read (with its 1/2-inch-tall LED numbers and measurements out to two decimal places), it also rotates the display if the angle finder is needed in an upside-down position so you can easily read it. It also has a button to turn on a screen backlight if it's too dark to read the dimensions under the car, and arrows on each end of the display to tell you which end is up and which end is down.

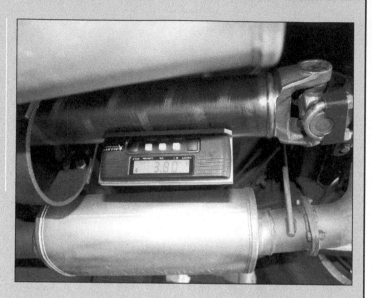

The digital angle finder does the exact same job as the analog version, but is easier to read due to its digital readout. It costs a bit more money, but it saves time and effort when checking critical angles.

to roll the pinion upward and then roll the entire rear end out of the car. This rear-end bracket and torque tube eliminates this condition. However, the stress transferred to the torque tube's attachment point on the transmission tailshaft housing very often cracks or breaks the transmission tailshaft housing or the bracket the torque tube attaches to at the rear-end housing.

Avid racers routinely searched salvage yards for spare brackets when these cars were newer. By monitoring the bracket for cracks at the race and with a spare bracket in hand, complete bracket failure could be avoided by replacing the bracket at the first sign of a crack. With only four bolts (two in the torque tube and two in the bracket), the part could be changed easily at the track in just a few minutes.

The powdercoated chrome-moly torque tube comes with a beefier rear mount and a much-improved front

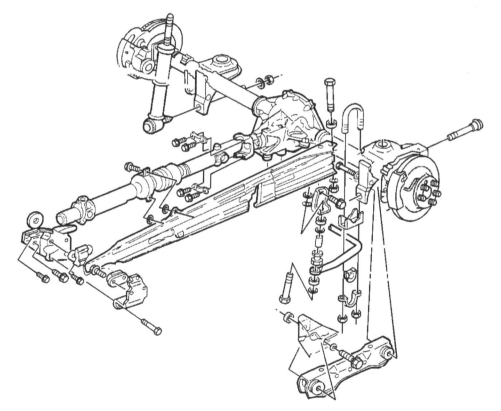

This exploded-view drawing shows all the major components from the GM F-Body three-link rear suspension system used on third- and fourth-gen cars. The single torque arm is clearly visible, extending forward from the rear axle housing to the transmission tailshaft.

This factory F-Body three-link torque arm mount is shown looking back from the front. The transmission tailshaft is leaking all over it. Look at the brackets holding it in place, and the general design of the stamped-steel arm. The materials are relatively light and will bend or flex under the high stress drag racing brings with it.

This is the rear mount of the same three-link factory torque arm. You can see the rear axle to the right.

1. Drive the front tires onto the scale as close to the center of the scale as possible without getting the rear tires onto the scale.
2. Have the scale read while you are still in the car, giving you the car's front-end weight.
3. Once you have that weight, drive all four tires onto the scale and get the car's total weight with the driver in place.
4. Drive the car forward until the front tires are off the scale and the rear tires as close to the center of the scale as possible. Have that weight recorded, again with the driver in the car.
5. To double check the accuracy of the various weights, you should be able to add the "front only" weight to the "rear only" weight and be within a few pounds of the "total car" weight.

mount with a 3/4-inch heim joint on the torque tube for strength and maximum freedom of movement when attached to the new front mount. Three-quarter-inch heim joints are used to attach the chrome-moly torque tube to the beefier rear bracket, which attaches to the rear-end housing.

The front mount looks similar to a rear leaf-spring shackle, which moves back and forth as the body rises or lowers. This allows the torque tube to freely get longer or shorter as the body raises or lowers on the chassis, thus removing most of the stress on the tailshaft housing and help prevent broken transmission cases. I have developed several mounts for many different transmission combinations.

Scale Procedure

If you have not four-corner scaled your car (covered in Chapter 10), take it to a commercial scale and follow this procedure:

Now you should be able to get your GM F-Body car on the track and be competitive in your class. As with any car, there is no single answer as to what works every time for every car. However, with the information in this chapter, you should have the necessary knowledge to make your car the best it can be.

REAR SUSPENSION: COIL SPRINGS AND FOUR-LINK

This chapter looks at muscle cars with rear suspension systems using coil springs with two upper and two lower control arms. These cars include GM intermediates built in 1964–1977 (A-Bodies), 1978–1988 (G-Bodies), 1994–1996 Impala SS cars (B-Bodies), and 1979–2004 Ford Mustangs (Fox-Bodies).

Rear-wheel-drive cars with rear coil springs and two upper and two lower control arms were designed to give a combination of maximum comfort, stability, and traction.

Unfortunately for the performance enthusiast, stability and traction gave way to comfort.

General Motors and Ford factory four-link suspensions are quite similar to a four-link style suspension in a tube-chassis racing car, except it is not adjustable and the control arms are not parallel from front to rear. The two upper control arms are angled with the two front mounts farther apart than the two rear mounts. The two lower control arms are angled–just the opposite with the two front mounts closer together than the two rear mounts. These opposing angles act like a track locator, keeping the rear end centered under the car.

Basic Design

With soft rubber bushings in each end of the control arms, a quiet suspension with a soft ride was achieved. These control arms are what hold the rear axle housing in the car. The front of the two lower control arms are attached to the frame rails and the rear of the

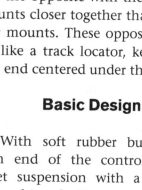

This is a typical GM mid-size car from the muscle car era—an Olds Cutlass, belonging to Canadian Tom Sheehan. Similar cars such as Chevy Chevelle, Buick Skylark, or Pontiac LeMans from 1964–1972 are referred to as A-Bodies.

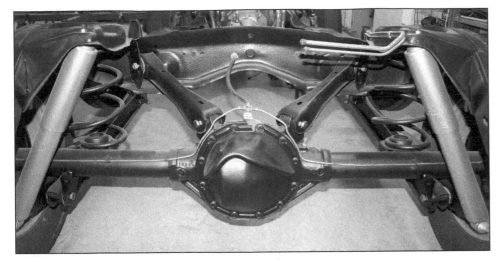

Shown is the factory four-link coil spring rear suspension from a typical GM A-Body. Note how there are two upper and two lower control arms, and how the uppers and lowers are mounted at very different angles.

This control arm from a Ford Mustang has a thick, soft-rubber bushing. Swapping these for stiffer polyurethane units makes a noticeable difference in launch performance, especially with a sticky tire on a well-prepared track surface.

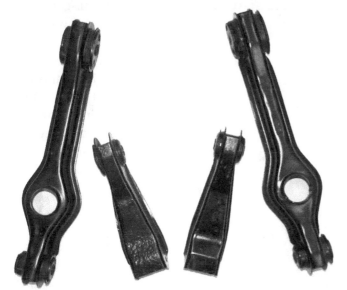

This is a complete set of factory control arms for the Fox-Bodied (post 1979) Ford Mustang. Like its GM counterparts, the Ford uses stamped-steel pieces, which are fine for stock applications on the street.

two lower control arms are attached to the axle housing. The front of the two upper control arms are attached to a crossmember welded 90 degrees to the frame rails and the rear of the upper control arms are attached to the rear-end housing. When one of these cars launch it tries to roll the pinion upward and roll the rear end out of the car. The upper con-trol arms keep this from happening. As it attempts to roll the pinion up, the upper control arms (which are attached to the crossmember) pull on the crossmember, preventing this from happening. Race cars with a lot of torque can and do flex this cross-member and eventually break it due to the flexing from repeated pulling and releasing. A piece of steel only flexes so many times before it even-tually cracks and breaks.

GM factory 4-speed cars came equipped with triangulation braces. These bars should be added to any GM rear-wheel-drive car with rear coil springs, two upper control arms, and two lower control arms. These 4-speed bars attach to the same bolts used at the front mount of the upper control arms down to the same bolts used at the front mount of the lower control arms. These stiffeners were appropriately named 4-speed bars since cars equipped with 4-speed manual transmissions launched much harder than those with automatic transmissions. With today's automatic transmissions and high-stall torque converters, an auto-matic-transmission car launches as quick and almost as hard as a man-ual-transmission car.

The 4-speed bars triangulated the two front upper control arm mounts with the frame attempting to elimi-nate the crossmember flex providing stiffness because of being attached to the frame. Although these 4-speed bars were better than none at all, they were just a bent piece of steel, which was not strong enough under race conditions. The factory 4-speed bars also had a slotted hole in one end for ease of installation that allowed for some crossmember movement.

Bushing Replacement

An upgrade to consider is to replace the control arm rubber bushings with polyurethane bushings by Energy Suspension. These greatly improve the handling of a car, whether it be hard cornering or just aggressive driving. All bushings in the upper and lower control arms, plus the two in the axle housing itself, must be replaced—for a total of eight. For ease of replacement, remove one arm at a time, complete the polyurethane bushing installation, then reinstall that arm before moving on to the next arm.

Control Arm Upgrades

I have never seen an upper control arm boxed-in from the factory, but it would be a good idea for a performance application. Be careful not to allow the steel boxing plate to interfere with the suspension travel or movement.

Boxed factory control arms with polyurethane bushings are also formed from thin mild steel and not rigid enough for heavy-duty drag racing applications. When it's time to upgrade, I suggest using tubular chrome-moly upper and lower control arms.

Using chrome-moly tubing and chrome-moly 3/4-inch adjusters, these arms have strength not found elsewhere. Even the heim joints are 3/4 inch for strength and they are bushed down to the bolt size needed. By having adjustable upper control arms, you are able to adjust pinion angle and chassis preload.

No-Hop Bars

All GM cars respond well to no-hop bars, which get their name from the fact that they eliminate wheel hop by causing the chassis to lift and push down harder on the tires. By raising the rear of the upper control arm and changing its angle, the car

Here's a look at the GM A-Body rear crossmember, as seen looking toward the rear of the car. The bolts seen passing through the crossmember are the pivot points for the upper control arms.

These GM triangulation bars are also called 4-speed bars. These serve to reinforce the pivot points of both the upper and lower arms by connecting them to each other.

The triangulation bar's slotted mount hole is clearly seen at the right. The factory arms are fairly rare, and are made of stamped steel.

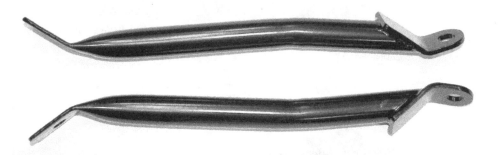

These aftermarket triangulation bars are made of tubular steel and are fully welded. They are much stronger than factory verions and readily available from several suppliers.

This is a factory stamped-steel control arm from a Ford Mustang. It's fine for a stock street car, but flexes under the added stress of drag strip launches.

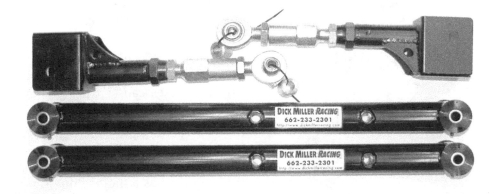

A matched set of tubular upper and lower control arms like these stiffen the entire rear suspension. Additionally, the upper arms are adjustable for length so they can be used to adjust preload in the suspension and pinion angle. They also come loaded with polyurethane bushings.

plants the rear tire harder and eliminates wheel hop. If the upper and lower control arms are extended farther forward, they eventually intersect. This imaginary intersection point determines whether the car lifts or squats in the rear when leaving the line.

Stay away from the cast-iron no-hop bars that have been on the market for years. They worked well with yesterday's low-horsepower cars, but they are too tall and can cause the upper control arm to hit the bottom of the trunk floor over the rear wheels on high-horsepower cars. By raising the rear of the upper control arm too far (shortening the imaginary intersection point to close to the rear end) the car hits the tire too hard. You can over power a tire causing it to wrap up like a rubber band. When it can't wrap any more it unwraps (like a spring) allowing the tire to unload and lose traction.

Because of this relatively radical action, the taller no-hop bars work some of the time at some tracks, but not all of the time at all tracks. For maximum strength correct-height (shorter) no-hop bars are made from 3/4-inch-thick laser-cut plate steel, not cast iron. They also have two mount holes to provide different mount points and further adjustment, although most racers only use the bottom hole.

Using no-hop bars requires a different adjustable upper control arm, since the angle is different.

On some of the earlier GM 12-bolt rears, the upper mounts were 1½ inches farther apart than the later, more typical axles. In order to use the early rear you would have to make some offset upper control arms. With my no-hop bars and adjustable upper control arm sets,

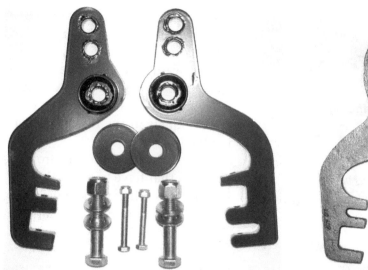

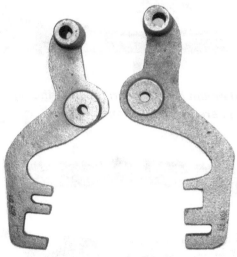

These no-hop bars were not designed well, and move the upper control arm too high compared to the stock location. Their quality was also relatively low, judging from the location of the holes through the casting. Avoid them.

This pair of no-hop bars for a GM rear axle change the angle of the upper control arms to eliminate wheel hop.

you can install one of the early 12-bolt rears into a later car. The upper control arm normally goes to the outside of the no-hop bar, but for this application the upper control arm may be moved to the inside of the no-hop bar, which is 3/4 inch different. Doing this on both sides

makes up the difference necessary to complete the installation (3/4 inch + 3/4 inch = 1½ inches).

You must install no-hop bars at an angle because of the center section design. There is some slop in the hole that the locating ring of the no-hop bar locates to, where the upper bushing used to be. This is not a problem. When you tighten the bolt holding the no-hop bar, it is not able to move. If you want to

decrease some of the slop, you can keep the steel sleeve around the outside of the bushing, cut it narrower (to match the width of the casting it came out of), and insert it from the opposite side before you bolt the flat plate in place. It sounds complicated, but it's simple once you see the parts involved.

No-hop-bar suspensions should only be used in cars equipped with a transmission brake or cars leaving the starting line at or near engine idle. That rules out turbo cars that need to spool up the turbo to get the engine speed (RPM) up where the turbo makes good boost unless the car has a transbrake.

Without a transmission brake, leaving the line with the engine RPM raised very far above idle while holding the brakes causes the car to lift in the rear before launching. The car loses part of the full suspension travel needed to plant the tires as hard as possible. What happens is that the car has a harder time transferring weight from the front to the rear (pitch rotation) since the rear of the car has already risen (transferring weight to the front of the car). If you wish to leave the line above idle, you

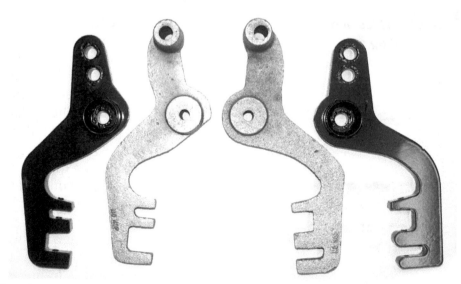

Here is a side-by-side look at a pair of "good" no-hop bars (on the outside) next to the "too tall" bars (on the inside). You can clearly see the differences, and also how the better-quality bolt-on bars have two location holes to choose from, versus the single hole atop the lower-quality cast bars.

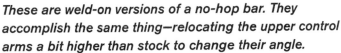

These are weld-on versions of a no-hop bar. They accomplish the same thing—relocating the upper control arms a bit higher than stock to change their angle.

Here is a no-hop bar with an adjustable upper control arm mounted in it. Once these components are added to the top of the rear axle housing, you can alter the suspension's performance to optimize it.

can experiment with the RPM level at which your car starts to lift in the rear by raising the idle a couple hundred RPM at a time and checking to see that the car does not lift in the rear at all when you put the car into gear from neutral. Keep doing that until you reach either the RPM you want and the car has not risen in the rear, or until the car starts to lift in the rear, in which case you need to lower the RPM.

Tubular lower control arms should come cross drilled with tubes welded in place to mount a sway bar for non drag race applications (see Chapter 10). Sway bars should not be used in drag race applications. Fixed-length lower control arms are recommended for applications up to 450 hp. Once cars approach 600 hp, adjustable lower control arms are recommended.

Adjustable lower control arms allow the rear axle housing to be properly squared in the car's chassis, which allows the car to roll more easily and therefore accelerate faster down the quarter-mile. They also allow the axle to be moved forward or rearward, which sometimes allows for a larger rear tire to be installed. If you move the car's rear axle in either a forward or rearward direction, be sure to check your driveshaft for proper end play. A minimum of 3/4 inch to a maximum of 1 inch of driveshaft end play needs to be maintained.

Track Locators

A car with heim joints in both the upper and lower control arms needs the axle to stay perfectly centered under the car. Diagonal braces exist for the lower control arms which act like a track locater that keep the housing centered. The track locaters attach to the lower control arm (approximately halfway back) and angle toward the center section. They attach to clamps bolted around the axle tubes as close to the center section as possible.

In testing with cars pushing 1,000 hp or more, quarter-mile ETs were reduced by up to .3 second using this setup with the diagonal braces. The reason for this reduction in ET was that the rear axle in the car now stays in a straight line while the car moves down the track instead of swinging side-to-side under the car. This same track locator can be used on lower control arms with holes in them for rear sway bar mounting.

Lift Bars

Ford Mustangs seem to respond better with what is referred to as lift bars. These lift bars work by lowering the rear mount point of the lower control arms. By contrast, GM cars

If you team the upper components with a solid lower control arm like this one, be prepared to hit the track a lot harder. Note the stock sway bar mount holes have been retained in this lower arm for GM A-Bodies.

respond better to raising the rear of the upper control arms using no-hop bars. From the factory, both the Ford and GM cars had different lengths and angles on their respective control arms and thus different imaginary intersection points.

Control Arm Adjustments

Once all four control arms are in place, it is time to adjust the upper control arms. Solid lower arms are built to the same length as the factory arms they replace. If you are using adjustable lower control arms they should be installed at the same length as the factory arms. If you wish to move the rear axle forward or back, both lower control arms must be set to the same length whether it be longer or shorter. If you discover that it is necessary to change them for alignment purposes, you need to reset the upper arms again. Do not install the diagonal track locater arms until all four control arms are set to the length you want.

If you are not using no-hop bars, both upper control arms should be adjusted to the same length as the factory arms they replace. If you

are using no-hop bars you should remove one upper control arm at a time to install them.

To adjust the upper control arms and pinion angle, please refer to Chapter 3 under the heading "Pinion Angle" on page 28.

Setting Preload

Now set the preload by shortening the passenger-side upper control arm and then locking those jamnuts into place. These cars usually drive to the right. Shortening the passenger-side upper control arm builds preload into the suspension and makes the car leave straight. For cars in the 400-hp range, I suggest one full turn (or six flats, as the adjuster has six sides). Higher-horsepower cars may need up to two turns (or 12 flats). Make a pass to evaluate the changes. If the car still turns toward the right, shorten the passenger-side upper control arm farther. If it turns to the left, lengthen the passenger side upper control arm. Make changes in one or two flat increments at a time. Too big of a change does not allow you to discover the best-possible setting.

It is preferred to use double-adjustable adjusters, meaning no bolts need to be removed to make adjustments. Just loosen the jamnuts to make adjustments as the adjuster has left-hand threads on one end and right-hand threads on the other end. Turning the adjuster is all that's required to lengthen or shorten a given control arm. Be sure to look at the threads when loosening the jamnuts so that you are not accidentally tightening them.

By comparison, single-adjustable arms require one end of the control arm to be removed to make adjustments. This makes the tuning process more difficult, especially with the upper control arms, since they're difficult to access and can be hard to remove and reinstall.

As discussed in Chapter 3, the best way to be certain of what is happening is to mark the steering wheel with a white or contrasting stripe at 12 o'clock (with the front wheels straight) and videotape your launch. After reviewing the video it is very apparent whether the steering wheel is turned right or left to correct a less-than-desirable launch.

Checking Driveshaft End Play

Having the proper driveshaft length is critical to maintaining correct end play. You need just enough to remove the driveshaft from the car, but you always want to have the maximum engagement of splines into the transmission for optimal strength. Here's how to measure it properly:

1. Unbolt the driveshaft, and slide it all the way into the transmission.
2. Draw a line with a felt-tip pen on the slip yoke next to the transmission tailshaft housing slip-yoke seal.

3. Bolt the driveshaft back into place.
4. Draw another line on the slip yoke next to the transmission tailshaft housing slip-yoke seal.

The distance between the two lines (perferably 3/4 to 1 inch) is the amount of driveshaft end play the car has. If you moved the rear axle forward, you probably need to shorten the driveshaft. If you moved the rear axle rearward you probably need to have a new driveshaft made, as they cannot be lengthened.

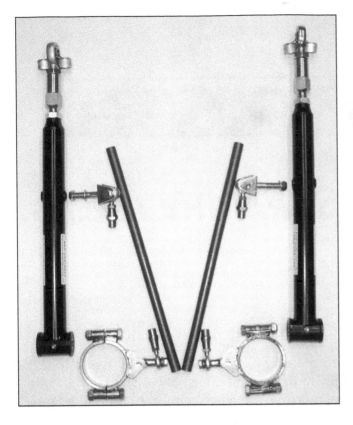

Once installed, the track locator setup looks like this. The rear axle can no longer flex from side-to-side.

This track locator kit is complete with a pair of adjustable-length lower control arms. The round brackets bolt to the rear axle housing, and then the lower arms connect to them.

Adjusting Preload

Cars without adjustable upper control arms need a stronger and/or taller spring on the rear passenger side than on the rear driver-side to set preload. Air bags can also accomplish this in cars with 400 hp or less. Normally, about 5 psi of air pressure in the driver-side air bag or no air bag at all on the driver's side, and 25 psi of air in the passenger-side air bag is enough to make the car launch straight. If the car turns right upon launch, add air to the passenger-side air bag. If the car turns left upon launch, remove air from the passenger-side air bag.

Both of these solutions (using a stronger spring on the passenger's side or using air bags) on four-link suspensions with non-adjustable rear upper control arms compensate for preload and partially get rid of wheel hop. But

they leave no method of setting pinion angle. Cars with adjustable upper control arms should not use either of these methods, as the preload is controlled with the adjustable upper control arms. Cars with adjustable upper control arms should use springs with equal strength on both sides.

Cars with no-hop bars should lift in the rear. Cars with no-hop bars and adjustable upper control arms should use rear springs of equal length and strength.

A car that lifts in the rear should use taller and lighter weight springs in the rear in order to compensate for the fact that they are lighter in weight and in strength.

A car that has lighter-tension springs lift farther and faster than a car that has heavier-tension springs. As you remove 100 pounds from a lighter spring, it lifts farther and

faster than removing 100 pounds from a heavier spring.

Never use ladder bars with a factory style four-link rear suspension. The upper and lower control arms (if extended forward) eventually reach an imaginary intersection point, which is the pivot point of the rear end. Ladder bars add a second pivot point (at the front of the ladder bar mount). The two opposing pivot points bind up the rear suspension. Therefore, they do get rid of wheel hop; however, the rear suspension becomes bound up and stiff and can't lift or squat. This does not allow any weight transfer (pitch rotation).

If you stick with the factory style four-link set up and these discussed additional modifications, it will not be necessary to alter your original car to achieve runs well into the 7-second-range quarter-mile ET.

FRONT SUSPENSION: STRAIGHT AXLES

This chapter discusses front suspensions with straight axles utilizing leaf springs. These suspensions have fixed caster and camber, but toe can be adjusted just as with the strut or A-arm front suspensions. This style suspension was very popular in the early days of drag racing, particularly in the Gasser classes, due to its weight-saving advantage. Today, even though it's had major improvements over the years, this style of front suspension is hardly ever used except for nostalgia or exhibition drag race cars. There are even clubs that exist just for the preservation of the vintage-style straight-axle Gasser and altered-wheelbase cars.

Typically, today thought of as "old school," leaf-sprung and straight-axle front suspensions have experienced a resurgence in the past few years as a result of the growth of the nostalgia drag race craze. In the 1960s, before the auto industry made the wholesale change to independent front suspensions, nearly all cars and trucks used the same style of steering and suspensions. Cast-steel-beam axles and leaf springs were common, easily serviced, and cheap. So, it was only natural that the hot rodders of the day used these pieces in their cars.

It goes without saying (as with anything mechanical) that all components need to be in good condition and repair status, as well as lubricated and maintained. Routine inspection for wear and damage, especially in the case of a car that wheel stands or pulls the front wheels off the ground upon launch, is strongly suggested.

The Basics

Front axles were typically all of the same basic design, the main difference being the physical size and, correspondingly, the weight. Truck axles were available, and for the abuse absorbed they were used in many of the dirt-track jalopy racers of the time. Drag racers were always looking for a weight advantage and sought out the lighter passenger car axles from Ford, Chevrolet, and Willys. These axles, with simple leaf springs, made a cheap and effective front suspension and steering package.

Weight Transfer

In order to assist in weight transfer, many racers of the day customized their spring packages by reducing the number of leaves in the pack, then

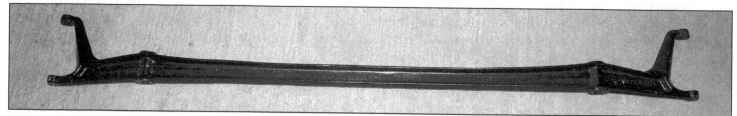

The Fords of the 1920s used a single-leaf spring, mounted parallel with the solid I-beam axle, to support the vehicle weight. This system was primitive, but functional.

This early Chevy II has received a straight axle and leaf springs to nail the vintage drag racer look. Credit goes to Don's Speed Shop for the nice work.

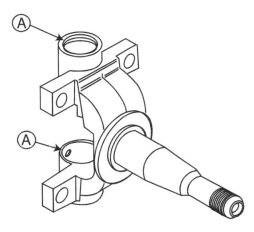

The early spindle/kingpin setups were basic and functional. The ball joints were installed in the upper and lower axle bosses.

A peek underneath a tube-axle-equipped hot rod shows the simplicity of the design. In this case, the leaf springs have been mounted 90 degrees from the direction of the axle. This is much stronger but still offers little comfort on rough roads.

had the remaining leaves arched or curved to an almost extreme amount. It's a pretty good bet these suspension systems did little for ride quality. They did accomplish what they wanted, which was to move the nose of the car upward, thus transferring weight to the rear tires and hoping the racing slicks gained traction. While it was only marginally effective, it was an improvement, so it

became a trend. The nose-up stance became representative of the time.

The next step of the progression was to reduce the weight of the front end. Due to the weight of an original-equipment-style beam axle, some forward thinkers decided a round tube could work as a substitute. Chassis builders of the day were soon making heavy-wall tubing, with bosses welded to the ends that accepted orig-

inal-equipment-style spindles. Typically, the Ford spindle was chosen for weight considerations. The tube axle was born, and then the straight axle. Chassis/axle builders were turning these things out as quickly and cheaply as possible. A straight piece of tubing with the ends welded on was an easy out the door product. Put the correct length of tube in a jig, secure the ends, use a stick welder—and presto, a race car axle was born. With the added benefit of the straight piece of tubing giving a bit more lift to the front end of the car, there could be a reduction in the weight of the spring package by reducing the number of leaves needed to get the stance desired. Less weight means you go faster.

It was believed that a higher front end allowed for quicker weight transfer, thus giving more traction and allowing the car to get going faster. This isn't all true, of course, but it was believed then.

Camber

The front-end alignment was of secondary importance in this system. The primary concern for the racer was high-speed stability. The camber angle was predetermined and pretty well fixed when the ends were welded to the tube.

Camber relates to the wheels being perpendicular, or straight up and down. If the wheel leans in at the top, toward the frame, it has negative camber. If the wheel leans outward at the top, away from the frame, it has positive camber. For maximum straight-line acceleration, the camber angle should be near zero so that the entire tread (the tire) is flat on the road. Positive or negative camber has a scrubbing effect due to the tire being at an angle, and increases rolling resistance. Near zero camber helps the car accelerate more quickly, as do narrow tires, which have less rolling resistance. The only camber adjustment method available on straight axles is to physically bend the axle. Heavy truck and trailer shops are equipped to do this by securing the axle to a fixed point while applying pressure with a hydraulic ram.

Caster

Caster deals with the spindle location governed by the upper and lower ball joints. Caster (unlike camber and toe, which are viewed from the front or rear of the car) is viewed from the side of the car. Caster may be set with each side independent from the other. For street driving, caster usually has negative 1/2 degree of caster on the left side to compensate for the crown built into most roads for water runoff. The side of the car with the least amount of caster pulls toward that side. On drag race cars running down a level track, the caster should be the same on both sides. Greater caster angles improve straight-line stability, but they also cause an increase in steering effort. In a typical street car, the

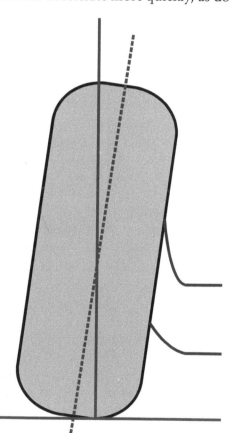

Negative camber is when the wheel is tipped inward at the top. If the top of the wheel points outward, away from the chassis, it has positive camber.

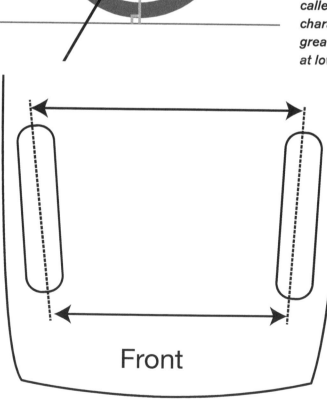

Front

The angle between the upper and lower balljoints is called caster. The steering characteristics are affected greatly by caster, especially at low speeds.

Toe is defined as the distance between the front of the tires compared with the distance between the rear of the tires. A little toe-in helps keep the car moving straight down the road. Too much causes premature tire wear. Too little may result in a car that likes to wander instead of traveling straight.

normal range of positive caster is 3 to 5 degrees, but lower settings can be used on heavier vehicles to keep the steering effort reasonable.

Viewed from the side, draw an imaginary line from the top mounting point for the spindle (ball joint) to the lower mounting point for the spindle (ball joint). Caster is the number of degrees (positive or negative) front to back from this vertical line. If the top ball joint is more rearward than the bottom ball joint, the caster is positive. If the ball joint is tilted forward, the caster is negative. Positive caster tends to straighten the wheel when the vehicle is traveling forward, and thus is used to enhance straight-line stability. That is why after turning, your steering wheel slowly returns to center without any correction from you. It's not usually as quick returning to a straight forward direction as we want so we give it some help by turning the steering wheel back to the straight-ahead position.

With straight axles, positive caster (king pin inclination) is the ticket for stability. A typical Gasser setting starts at 7 degrees and is fine-tuned to as much as 10 degrees. Adjustments are done by placing a wedge between the spring and the axle/spring mounting pad, just like setting pinion angle in a rear-wheel-drive car with leaf springs in the back.

These settings are typical of full-bodied cars. Look at the front end of a front-engine dragster with a straight axle. The positive caster for one of these cars is so extreme (starting at 25 degrees) that in many cases, when the wheels are at their full left or right extension, they cannot be returned to straight without an assist from a crewmember physically grabbing the tire and straightening it to neutral (straight-forward facing).

The basic push-pull steering system used in the early Fords (among others) was subject to bump steer. When you hit a bump in the road, the suspension's travel caused the wheels to move left or right—obviously quite dangerous.

Toe

The final aspect of the alignment dilemma is toe, which refers to the wheels being parallel with each other, forward to backward (tracking). Toe has a great impact on stability at speed. While you'd think that setting toe to 0 would be perfect and offer the least resistance, that is not the case. Alignment shops set up most muscle-era drag cars with 1/8-inch toe-in so the front edges of the tires are 1/8-inch closer to each other than the rear edges of the tires. If the rear edges of the tires are closer to each other, instead of the front edges, it is called toe-out. The reason for 1/8-inch toe-in is that at 60 to 80 mph (a somewhat arbitrary number), the wind rushing at the front of the car tries to push the front of the tires apart. Setting the toe-in at 1/8-inch is like preloading the rear suspension. It offsets the wind resistance so as the car goes faster and faster, the wheels deflect to 0 toe-in and are straight (parallel) with each other.

Toe settings effect tire wear as well. For minimum tire wear and power loss, the wheels should point straight ahead (0 toe-in) as the car is moving in a straight line at highway speed. Too much toe-in causes the tires' outside edges to wear, while too much toe-out causes the tires' inside edges to wear. As not all cars attain the same speeds on the quarter-mile tracks, or even on eighth-mile tracks, the settings for each car may need to be different.

Gasser Era

Chuck Lipka of the Geezer Gassers says his car utilizes toe-out. With the front end already up in the air at the starting line (typical Gasser setting), then as the front end rises farther on acceleration, the tires/wheels want to return to a straight-ahead or neutral setting. As the car continues to accelerate and the weight continues to transfer rearward with even more air rushing under the car, the tire contact patch is reduced and lessens the scuff factor. Remember, these cars begin the run with the front end up in the air, not like today's muscle cars with the

A Bit of History

The classic American hot rod era lasted from 1945 to about 1965. Classic hot rods required significant modification by their owners. Hot rods were built on a variety of old, often historic, car models. Cars manufactured before 1945 were considered ideal fodder for hot rod transformations because their bodies and frames were often in good shape, while their engines and transmissions needed to be replaced. This was exactly what hot rod enthusiasts wanted since it allowed them to install more reliable and powerful engines such as the flathead Ford V-8 (circa 1932–1954) or later on the Chevrolet V-8 (circa 1955–present).

One of the more popular Gassers was known as the T-bucket because it was based on the Ford Model T. The stock Ford suspension on the front of the Model T consisted of a solid I-beam front axle (a dependent suspension), a U-shaped buggy spring (leaf spring), and a wishbone-shaped radius rod with a ball at the rear end that pivoted in a cup attached to the transmission.

Ford engineers built the Model T to ride high with a large amount of suspension movement, which was an ideal design for the rough, primitive roads of the 1930s. After World War II, hot rodders began experimenting with larger Cadillac- or Lincoln-based V-8 engines, which meant that the wishbone-shaped radius rod was no longer applicable. Instead, they removed the center ball and bolted the ends of the wishbone to the frame rails. This

The early Ford Model T remains a popular choice among hot rodders. What it takes to lower one of these straight-axle front suspensions and make it work well has been heavily researched and refined in the 100-plus years since these cars were produced.

split wishbone design lowered the front axle about 1 inch and improved vehicle handling.

Lowering the axle more than 1 inch required a brand-new design. Throughout the 1940s and 1950s, Bell Auto offered dropped tube axles that lowered the car a full 5 inches. Tube axles were built from smooth, steel tubing and balanced strength with improved aerodynamics. The steel surface also accepted chrome plating better than the forged I-beam axles, so hot rodders often preferred them for their aesthetic qualities as well.

Some hot rod enthusiasts, however, argued that the tube axle's rigidity and inability to flex compromised how it handled the stresses of driving. To accommodate this, hot rodders introduced the four-bar suspension, using two mounting points on the axle and two on the frame. At each mounting point, aircraft-style rod ends provided plenty of movement at all angles. The result? The four-bar system improved how the suspension worked in all driving conditions.

Splitting the single suspension arm (called a wishbone) resulted in a better functioning, lowered single front axle. The resulting "split wishbone" suspension has become a standard upgrade in the world of early hot rods and street rods.

front end aerodynamically down for less air resistance and drag.

Steering Styles

Straight-axle suspensions have two distinctly different styles of steering. Both styles accomplish the same thing, but with different approaches.

Original System

Cars using a straight axle from the 1930s and 1940s typically used a steering box and Pitman arm working forward-to-backward (or push-and-pull). This in turn acted on a relay rod that connected the Pitman arm to a steering arm, or knuckle, that moved the left spindle assembly to the left or right. The left spindle was then connected to the right spindle with an adjustable tie rod that transferred the same steering inputs to each wheel so they worked together. The steering box is typically mounted to the left frame rail, and the connection to the steering arm runs parallel to the frame rail (front to rear).

Cross Steer

The other system, and the better choice in the eyes of many, is the cross-steer arrangement. In this style, the steering box mounts to the left frame rail. The Pitman arm connects to the right spindle/steering arm with a relay rod. The right spindle is then connected to the left spindle with a tie rod. This system all but eliminates the bump steer dilemma, especially when the alignment specs of positive caster and toe-in are in sync.

The challenge with cross-steer setups is keeping the relay rod and the tie rod parallel to each other as much as possible, as well as parallel to the ground. When the steering is moved through its full range left to right, the relay rod and the tie rod should remain on the same plane. Placement of the steering box is the key to attaining this specification. If the steering box is too far forward, the relay rod and tie rod can come in contact and in extreme cases they cross.

In a worst-case scenario, the steering momentarily binds or locks up. Then as you apply more steering-wheel pressure to overcome the lockup, the relay rod and the tie rod overcome the bind and the steering wheel is jerked out of your hands, stopping at a full-turn lock. Definitely not a good situation.

Bump Steer

These steering systems worked in their day with low speeds, narrow tires, marginally adequate road surfaces, and light overall vehicle weights (especially in the front). The main concern and complaint with this type of system is a problem known as bump steer. The systems are susceptible to dramatic and sometimes unexpected, possibly violent jerking of the steering wheel when the wheel/tire strikes a pothole or a bump in the pavement surface. With the steering box and Pitman arm moving front to rear, striking a pothole or bump transfers in full force directly to the steering wheel. It gets worse with any degree of wear in the front end (such as worn tie rod ends, kingpins, steering box, etc.).

Front Tires

For drag racing, the narrower the front tire, the better. However, don't get into a situation where safety is an issue because your tires are not rated in a high enough capacity for your car's weight. Too narrow of

Here's a good look at a cross-steer system, which was a great improvement over the older push-pull design. This is a more modern car being built to resemble the vintage drag cars of the 1950s and 1960s, so the best-possible performance is being engineered into it while keeping the style of the older cars.

a tire on too narrow of a rim in an extreme handling situation (other than straight forward) could cause the tire to collapse, unseat, or come off the rim.

Mickey Thompson makes a narrow front tire in several different sizes that can be mounted on 4-inch-wide rims. They are available in eight-ply to hold up on heavy drag cars. These front tires are Department of Transportation (DOT) approved and therefore may be used on the street for those with dual-purpose street/strip cars. Mickey Thompson and Moroso also make a non-DOT-approved front tire that is much lighter in weight (13 pounds).

Since I occasionally drive my car to a cruise-in, I prefer the DOT-approved tires. Both the approved and non-approved tires have a crowned tread, so that under acceleration while the car is experiencing weight transfer (pitch rotation) the amount of tread on the pavement becomes less and offers even less rolling resistance. These tires are bias-ply designs and are not recommended by the manufacturer to be used with radial tires in the rear.

When choosing any non-original-equipment tires, it's important to match the front tires as close as possible to the rear tires. Changing the stance of the car to where the front of the car is lower than the rear of the car greatly hinders weight transfer (pitch rotation), as it makes the front of the car heavier and much harder to lift for maximum weight transfer.

Smaller-diameter front tires can also be compensated for through spring selection. Smaller-diameter front tires can create better reaction times, but slower 60-foot times. The opposite is true in larger-diameter front tires—they give you slower reaction times with quicker 60-foot times.

With this chapter's information you now understand the dynamics of using a straight-axle front end. In the Gasser days they were easily available and lightweight. With today's tech-

This Mickey Thompson DOT-approved front tire offers minimal rolling resistance and an aerodynamic shape. Don't expect it to handle well on hard corners though.

nology, race cars with straight-axle front ends are outdated and almost non existent, except for nostalgia racing.

Moroso also offers a fine-quality front tire in many different heights and widths. It's not DOT-approved for street use. Run the tallest tire you can because larger front tires create a bigger measureable rollout distance, which makes for a quicker 60-foot time but a slower reaction time. In this case, the pros typically outweigh the cons.

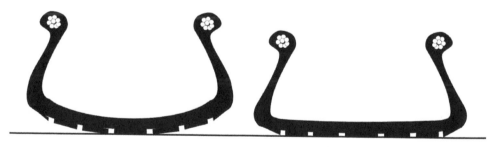

This image illustrates why the rounded tread design (left) of drag-specific tires is preferred. There is less rubber on the ground, which means less rolling resistance. This is also why these tires cannot be expected to perform well around corners.

The Geezer Gassers

Enthusiast and member Chuck Lipka gave me the low-down on The Geezer Gassers:

"The group was formed (unofficially) in 1996. The Goodguys Vintage Racing Association was our base and its race director was an old timer who liked our cars and the idea of heads-up racing to the finish line, as opposed to bracket racing. The first event we were invited to was the NHRA Bowling Green Hot Rod Reunion, and we have been regulars ever since.

"The group currently has 36 members, primarily from the Midwest. The cars are all period-correct for the 1960s look with the nose up, straight axles, paint, and graphics. They run the gamut in make, styles, colors, and powertrains.

"Due to the wide variety of powertrains our program is now set up on an index basis. We run 1/2-second breaks from 9.50 to 12.0. Most of the cars run the 10-second index, with six or eight of them in the 9-second range. Powertrains are most commonly small-block or big-block Chevy based. We do have some orphan engines competing, like big- and small-block Fords, several Chrysler Hemis, my Oldsmobile, and even a 472-ci Cadillac.

"The group has a huge emphasis on safety. All the cars run engine 'diapers' no matter how fast or slow. Any car that is capable of launching 'wheels up' has to have wheelie bars. Over half of the cars are chassis certified by NHRA.

"There is a self-imposed limit on performance of 9.50 seconds and 150 mph. These cars were erratic in their day, and superior tires and improved mechanical technology has made that even more of an issue today.

"Group rules include no electronics (beyond a transbrake and an electronic ignition/rev limiter), gasoline only, no body enhancements (wings, droop nose, raised quarter panels, etc.), and no nitrous oxide or nitromethane. Blowers are limited to being no larger than a 6-71."

Chuck's own Gasser (a 1947 Willys sedan) is a purpose built, 'glass bodied, original-chassis, Olds-powered car and was homebuilt. The Olds engine uses a Diesel block for the foundation. Internals include four-bolt billet steel main caps, a billet steel crank, aluminum rods, custom pistons, Engle cam, and Edelbrock heads, blower intake, and a 6-71 blower on top. The car's best ET so far is a 11.215 at 112 mph in the quarter-mile at Holly Springs, Mississippi, in October 2010.

Chuck Lipka's 1941 Willys Gasser runs a tubular front axle with a well-designed cross-steer setup. You can also see top-quality front tires and modern disc brakes. The front suspension maintains the vintage look while being safer overall.

FRONT SUSPENSION: DOUBLE A-ARM

Double A-arm front suspension cars are also referred to as double-wishbone suspensions. Either name is an accurate description of the parts being discussed in this chapter. I refer to them throughout this book as A-arms. Depending upon the vehicle, they can be rather flat and triangular shaped. Looking at the physical part itself, you can imagine either a wishbone from last Thanksgiving's turkey or the capitol letter "A," thus their name.

Since they are not part of the frame itself but attach to the main frame they are considered a subframe. The end of the "A" with two legs attaches to the frame and pivots, while the pointed end of the "A" attaches to the steering knuckle and pivots upon a ball joint. Two A-arms per wheel make up a double A-arm suspension. If your car has only one A-arm per wheel, usually the lower, then your car has a single A-arm, or MacPherson strut suspension (see Chapter 7). If the front wheels are connected by a rigid axle, the car has a dependent front suspension (see Chapter 5). If the front wheels move independently from each other, the car has an independent front suspension.

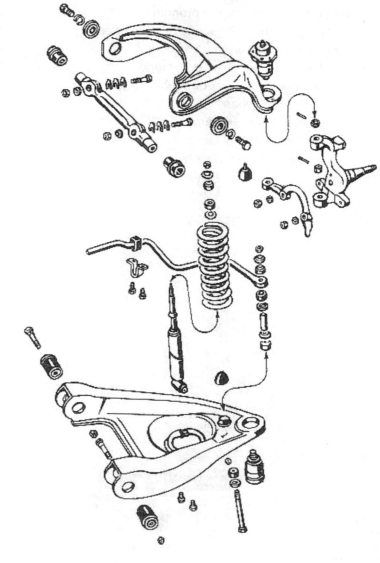

Here is an exploded view of a typical double A-arm front suspension. This was used as the standard design under most full-size American cars before the advent of MacPherson struts.

The lower control arm in a double A-arm suspension is a stamped-steel part that supports the coil spring and shock absorber, along with the lower ball joint. This is a GM A-Body part.

Here are both upper and lower control arms from a GM A-Body. The upper arm does not have to support the spring or the shock, as does the lower arm, so it can be lighter.

While there are several different possible configurations, a double A-arm independent suspension typically uses two A-shaped arms to locate the wheel. Each side utilizes a shock absorber and a coil spring to absorb vibrations and bumps.

Double A-arm suspensions allow for more control over the camber angle of the wheel, which is the degree to which the wheels tilt in and out. They also help minimize roll or sway and provide a more consistent steering feel. Because of these characteristics, the double A-arm suspension is common on the front wheels of larger cars as well as most GM and Ford cars from the muscle car days.

Alignment

Three areas that need attention to align the wheels of a double A-arm independent suspension-equipped car are: caster, camber, and toe. The following is an explanation of these three settings as they pertain to a drag race car. Settings for street-driven cars are much closer to factory specifications.

Camber changes drastically as the suspension moves up or down when hitting bumps and potholes. This also occurs in a stock double A-arm independent suspension car doing a wheel stand, as the tires tilt in toward each other dramatically at the top. Typical body roll in such a car launching hard at the starting line lifts the driver-side tire 6 to 12 inches off the ground with the passenger side still on the ground. This can also dramatically influence camber.

For maximum straight-line acceleration, the camber angle should be near zero so that the tread is flat on the road. Positive or negative camber has a scrubbing effect (due to the tire being at an angle) and increases the rolling resistance. Significant suspension modifications like raising, lowering, or using dropped spindles may require camber adjustments. Near 0 camber helps the car accelerate quicker, as do narrow tires, which

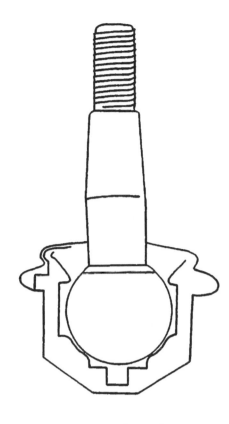

A typical ball joint allows the suspension to travel in any direction with a minimal amount of resistance. Ball joints require regular maintenance with fresh grease, and are designed to wear out over time since friction is engineered into them. When building a car for high performance, plan on replacing them to ensure you have fresh units in place.

have less rolling resistance. In this case, the narrower the tire, the better. However, don't get yourself into a situation where safety is an issue because your tires are not rated in a high enough capacity for your car's weight (see "Front Tires" on page 47 for more information about front tires specifically designed for drag racing).

If your front end is extremely worn or well used, the toe-in might be set as high as 1/4 inch. Since most race cars are pushed beyond the limits of normal street cars this may help you see the importance of maintaining your car's front-end components.

Now you can see that toe settings have a great impact on directional stability as well as tire wear. Besides continually checking the front steering components for wear and replacing them at the first sign of wear you should install polyurethane bushings in the A-arms where they attach to the frame. For a quieter and softer ride, manufacturers installed soft rubber bushings into A-arms. This allowed for movement when pushed to the limit. Race cars need to get rid of this mushy, comfortable, suspension-flexing ride by installing spherical bushings (heim joints), polyurethane, plastic, or metal bushings to provide optimum control of suspension links. That is why a street car requires more toe-in than a race car and a worn street car requires more toe-in than a

better condition street car.

Over the years with many potholes or speed bumps the frame and the crossmember below the engine can sag or become bent without the car ever being in an accident. Some vehicles therefore require occasional realignment.

Adjusting Settings

On double A-arm front suspensions, a car's camber or caster settings are changed by the placement of shims between the cross shaft (where the upper A-arm is mounted) and the frame. There are two studs pressed into the frame on each side. The cross shafts are loosened and horseshoe-shaped shims are slid over each stud and then retightened to make adjustments.

Camber is affected by adding or removing an equal number of shims from both studs. If you add shims to the shim pack, the top of the tire

moves inward, creating more negative camber. Removing shims from the shim pack tips the tire out at the top creating more positive camber.

Caster is changed by adding or removing different quantities of shims from both studs. Removing a shim from the front stud moves the upper ball joint out and back, creating more positive caster. Adding a shim to the front stud moves the upper ball joint in and forward, creating more negative caster. However, notice the words "in" and "out." Your camber setting also changes and may need to be reset. If you need a dramatic change you can take a shim off the front stud and add it to the rear stud. This adds more positive caster without changing camber.

Toe is changed by turning the threaded sleeves connecting the tie rod ends. Threading the tie rod longer creates toe-out. Threading the tie-rod ends shorter creates toe-in.

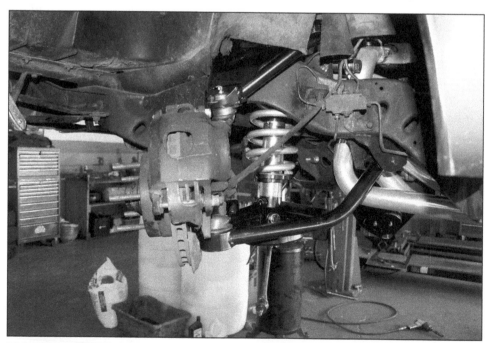

This GM A-Body vehicle has tubular upper and lower control arms and a hybrid coil-over conversion replacing the factory spring/shock combination. The coil-over does not support the full weight of the car, as the spring still uses the pocket in the chassis, hence the hybrid name.

The ride height with this QA1 coil-over conversion is adjustable using the threaded shock body, and the shock is adjustable using the knob at the bottom. QA1 offers these in both single-adjustable (shown) and double-adjustable versions.

Toe is set using a threaded sleeve on the steering tie-rod. This sleeve can be seen clearly at the bottom of this photo, extending inward from the bottom of the spindle in front of the lower control arm.

Chris and Linda Heminger's 1971 Olds Cutlass gets the wheels up more than a foot on launch. This is about the maximum height you'd ever want to achieve before the vehicle weight begins to transfer backward. At this level, it's still moving up and forward at the same time.

Each chassis needs different camber, caster, and toe settings. These settings are programmed into modern wheel-alignment machines by year, make, and model, and are updated periodically. Normally for drag racing cars, you want the tires as straight as possible. This translates to 0 camber and nearly 0 toe. With stock A-arms, go for as much positive caster as possible. Usually, you are limited to about 2 degrees. Offset upper control arm shafts are available through most distributors to provide an additional 1 to 2 degrees of positive caster. Most aftermarket upper control arms are set for 5 degrees of positive caster. Some chrome-moly upper control arms are adjustable and allow for as many degrees of positive caster as needed (such as those from Dick Miller Racing). In this case you should shoot for between 5 and 7 degrees of positive caster.

Toe measurements can be checked using a gauge similar to this one offered by Longacre. It is simply used as a reference point, and the distance between the tires is checked on the ground in front of and behind the front wheels. The difference in these measurements shows how much toe there is between the front wheels, if any.

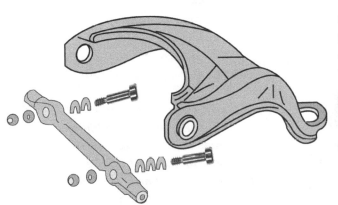

Camber and caster are set using stacks of shims on vehicles equipped with double A-arm suspensions. Adjusting the number of shims on the forward and rear upper A-arm mount bolts alters the angle of the arm to provide the desired caster and camber settings.

Sway Bars

The first improvement for cars with a front sway bar is to completely remove it for drag racing purposes.

Most performance-oriented double A-arm independent suspended cars have sway bars on the front to give the car additional handling stability. A sway bar is a round piece of steel that fastens to each frame rail and then to each lower A-arm which connects the driver's side of the suspension to the passenger's side. When the suspension on one side moves up or down the sway bar transfers movement to the other side. This keeps the car more level with less roll and better handling while reducing sway during hard cornering. Knowing how a sway bar works allows you to better understand why you don't want one on your drag race car. Be careful if your car is a dual purpose street/strip car. Depending on your driving style, you may need to re-install the sway bar when returning to the street.

By design, sway bars limit the travel of the front suspension and therefore don't allow enough front-end rise or weight transfer (pitch rotation), which is necessary to add down force to the rear tires and plant them as hard as possible. The more weight transfer, the better.

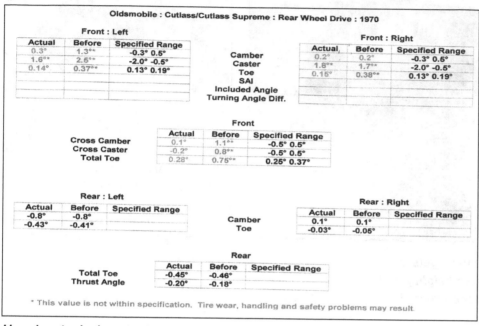

Oldsmobile : Cutlass/Cutlass Supreme : Rear Wheel Drive : 1970

Front : Left

Actual	Before	Specified Range				Front : Right		
0.3°	1.3°*	-0.3° 0.5°		Camber		Actual	Before	Specified Range
1.6°**	2.5°**	-2.0° -0.5°		Caster		0.2°	0.2°	-0.3° 0.5°
0.14°	0.37°**	0.13° 0.19°		Toe		1.6°**	1.7°**	-2.0° -0.5°
				SAI		0.15°	0.38°**	0.13° 0.19°
				Included Angle				
				Turning Angle Diff.				

Front

		Actual	Before	Specified Range
Cross Camber		0.1°	1.1°**	-0.5° 0.5°
Cross Caster		-0.2°	0.8°**	-0.5° 0.5°
Total Toe		0.28°	0.75°**	0.25° 0.37°

Rear : Left

Actual	Before	Specified Range				Rear : Right		
-0.8°	-0.8°			Camber		Actual	Before	Specified Range
-0.43°	-0.41°			Toe		0.1°	0.1°	
						-0.03°	-0.05°	

Rear

		Actual	Before	Specified Range
Total Toe		-0.45°	-0.46°	
Thrust Angle		-0.20°	-0.18°	

*This value is not within specification. Tire wear, handling and safety problems may result.

Here is a typical computer-generated alignment sheet from a modern shop. The car is placed on the alignment rack and reflectors are mounted to the wheels. Lasers are then used to determine the relative positions of the wheels in relation to each other. Trained technicians can then fine-tune the adjustments to bring the alignment into specifications.

If the vehicle cannot be brought into alignment specification, due to excessive wear, damage, or racing modifications, offset upper arm cross shafts like this one are available to provide as much as 2 degrees of additional positive caster.

Sway Bars versus Anti-Roll Bars

Most muscle cars came from the factory with front and/or rear sway bars. They are available direct fit with many aftermarket suppliers, in different diameters (bigger being stronger or lighter being weaker), and some are more universal. They are normally made from a solid round bar of steel shaped as needed for a particular application.

While road course cars and street driven only cars can benefit with the

These upper control arms (available from Hotchkis) have an additional 5 degrees of positive caster built into them for lowered vehicles. This minimizes the number of shims required to align the car.

These upper and lower tubular control arms for GM A-Body front suspensions are from Dick Miller Racing. They are much stronger than the factory arms, and the lower arms include an adapter so they can be used with either separate coil springs and shock absorbers, or aftermarket coil-over setups. Note the polyurethane coil insert in the lower arm's spring pocket as well.

Shown is a typical GM sway bar from an A-Body application. Other front sway bars are similar in design. The factory bars on these cars are solid steel, making them quite heavy. In a pure drag race application, it pays to remove them and save the weight. Their input on the suspension isn't required in straight-line acceleration.

use of sway bars, they should not be used on drag cars. They will get rid of a lot of the body movement or dipping in the corner in a hard turn. On a low-horsepower drag car they could be used to help with wheel hop. Notice I did not say get rid of wheel hop. Because of its design a sway bar never gets rid of a problem. It simply takes half of that problem and transfers it to the other side, such as with wheel hop. Taking half of the wheel hop problem and transferring it to the other side on a low horsepower car can make it seem like it has gone away. Going into a corner with a less than adequate spring and shock with a sway bar can add stability to the car.

If you are turning in the same direction all the time a stronger spring would be a better answer. If you are turning the car in both directions then a sway bar is mandatory. Muscle cars with front sway bars usually have the center section bolted to the frame and the ends are fastened to the steering arms. At the frame they are mounted inside rubber bushings to allow them to twist and flex, but in a minimal amount as compared with a car trying to do a wheelstand. In the 1970s, NHRA required Stock class cars that came from the factory with sway bar's to run them while racing in a Stock class. To get rid of the sway bar's tendency of limiting front suspension travel, some racers would ream out the rubber bushings to make them

Aftermarket sway-bar kits are readily available from a wide range of suppliers in both solid and tubular form. If you'd like to improve your car's handling, these are a good move. For drag racing applications, they aren't necessary.

almost useless. Since the rear sway bars were bolted directly to the lower control arms there wasn't much that could be done without leaving it off. Just as helping with wheel hop a rear sway bar hinders in trying to get individual corner tuning such as preload. It will fight the preload.

Anti-roll bars are not the same as sway bars. Anti-roll bars are used on drag cars to get rid of the typical body roll upon launch having the driver's side front tire about a foot higher off the ground than the passenger side tire.

Anti-roll bars, unlike sway bars, are made from round tubing instead of being solid steel. All of my anti-roll bars are chrome moly because of the demand needed of the anti-roll bar to twist and return to its original shape.

Using different methods, the anti-roll bar is fastened to the frame and each side of the rear end housing. By being welded to the frame rails, the anti-roll bar, upon launch, will push on the housing mounts and absorb the twisting from the car which is trying to raise the driver's side front wheel and then the anti-roll bar will use the passenger side of the frame as leverage to prevent this from happening, thus creating a launch which is level at the front of the car.

Shocks

As mentioned earlier, each side of a car utilizes a shock absorber and a coil spring to absorb vibrations and bumps. Good quality shocks are very important for today's higher horse-power cars. An inexpensive set of shocks like 90/10 or three way adjustable shocks should work on cars with as much as 300 to 350 hp.

If you have a car that does very high wheel stands, you can control how hard or soft the car comes back down on the ground. Too hard can cause the car to bounce back into the air repeatedly. That causes the rear tires to un-plant and then re-plant with each undulation. Not only is this hard on traction and ETs, it is also hard on driveline parts. Where you are in the torque band determines just how bad the effect is. As the tire unloads, the converter with less load stalls to a lower RPM as the engine spins to a higher RPM. This action makes achieving an accurate dial-in impossible.

With most front-adjustable shocks, the best setting to start with is near the middle of however many adjustments the shock has. If your car needs more front end lift (pitch rotation), a softer setting is needed. If your car's front end is raising too far, a firmer setting is needed.

As mentioned in other chapters, adequate shock travel is essential. Measure the total amount of suspension travel between fully compressed and fully extended without a shock or spring in place to determine the amount of suspension travel you have. Then specify a shock absorber capable of extending and compressing within those limits. A shock that bottoms out or extends fully before the suspension travel arc is reached inevitably bounces back when it reaches its limit. This generates unpredictable results—dangerous in a racing situation. Don't let this happen to you. Measure carefully, consult with your shock manufacturer, and get the proper components in place.

This car definitely needs an anti-roll bar to get rid of the body roll. This much body roll will plant the passenger-side rear tires harder than the driver's side tires, resulting in a crooked launch and a 60-foot time not what it should be. Depending on how rigid the roll cage is, that much body roll could also damage some body panels and glass.

This ladder-bar car is hitting the rear slicks way too hard as shown by the sidewall folding under the tire into the tread (wadding). Several things could be wrong. The rear tire needs more air and the ladder bars are set too aggressive; plus the rear shocks should be tighter on extension.

Not only does your car go faster, but your life may depend on it!

Measuring For Shocks

Companies such as QA1 have shocks for most muscle car applications. Just as it is up to an engine builder to be sure all machine work and all parts measure to the spec necessary for the job, it is your responsibility to be sure your shocks have the right measurements to suit your car's needs. Therefore, you must take three measurements for your car and compare them to the measurement of the shocks you are about to use. Shocks are necessary on your car to control the car's suspension (see sidebar "Proper Shock Length is Critical" on page 13). However, if the shock runs out of travel in either direction

your suspension movement will stop abruptly and control will be lost.

To dimensionally check your car's shock needs, you must get the measurement for the car's shock compressed, extended, and ride height lengths. In order to verify the correct shock by length for your vehicle, the following procedure can be used. This way you can be sure your shock won't bottom out or top out by comparing the measurements you get either with the shock listed for your car or go to the shock companies tables and pick the one to suit your car's needs.

The shock's measurement at ride height is usually all that is needed. However, some shock companies only publish compressed and extended measurements. If you are using this

method then you need your car's actual ride height to be somewhere in the middle or so that there is minimally more travel on the extension side as opposed to the compressed side. Then call your favorite shock supplier (like me) and buy a shock with the same recommended ride height. However, my belief of not taking anyone else's work for granted or as being right prevents me from stopping there. To get these measurements for the car's shock compressed, extended, and ride height length you need to take the following measurements from the car's chassis.

First raise the vehicle off the ground and let the suspension and wheels hang freely. Remove the shocks and carefully allow the suspension to drop as far as it can, being sure your are not damaging any connected brake lines. Measure from the center of the upper shock mount to the center of lower shock mount. This measurement is the car's maximum necessary extended shock length. Place the car completely back on the ground, resting on all four tires. Now remeasure from the center of the upper shock mount to the center of lower shock mount. This is your ride height.

Next measure from the bump stop to where the bump stop contacts. The bump stops may be different from the front of the car to the rear of the car. Subtracting the bump stop travel measurement from the ride height measurement you now have the compressed measurement. Shocks are measured from the center of loops and/or shock shaft/ stud shoulders. The measurements are taken from mounting surface to mounting surface.

Now determine the upper and lower mounting type and size.

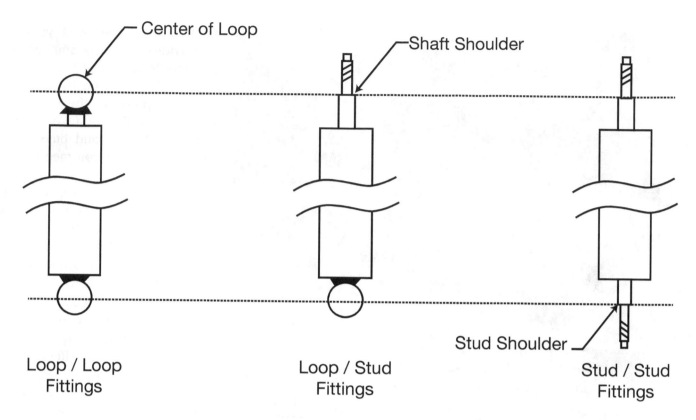

Left: When measuring shocks with loops or eyes on each end, the length measurement is measured from the center of the loop on one end to the center of the loop on the other end. Middle: When measuring shocks with a stud on one end and a loop on the other end, the length measurement is measured from the shaft shoulder to the center of the loop on the other end. Right: When measuring shocks with a stud on both ends, the length measurement is measured from the shaft shoulder on one end to the shaft shoulder on the other end.

For loop mounts, the inside bolt hole diameter is needed. For cross pin mounts, the bolt hole size is needed, as well as the distance between bolt holes. Quite often the ends you need may not be offered in the size you need, but normally I can change the shock from one type end to another style.

Spring Selection

Front-spring selection is very important yet very simple. Your car needs the lightest spring available that will hold the car at the desired ride height. That usually requires a lighter-weight and taller front spring. Using a lighter-weight spring than factory causes the spring to col-lapse farther than the factory spring. You therefore need a taller spring to keep the front end at normal ride height.

With a lighter-weight spring being compressed farther, the spring has stored (potential) energy, which causes the front of the car to lift quicker and farther during hard acceleration and weight transfer (pitch rotation). As the weight transfer begins removing 200 pounds from a lighter-weight and taller spring it gives more rise to the car than removing 200 pounds from a heaver-weight and shorter spring.

Moroso has a good selection of front drag-race-specific coil springs, which satisfy the needs of most of the original muscle cars at the race tracks. Even then, the help of a good educated guess helps. On the other hand, nothing works better than having your car weighed.

If you have not four-corner scaled your car, take your car to a scale. Usually a recycle yard or a grain elevator or your own race track has scales accurate enough for this task. The proper procedure for weighing your car is detailed on page 102. Once you're armed with the car's total weight and know how it's divided between the front and rear, you're well-armed to outfit the car with the best-possible components. Get all the information you can before consulting with an expert and purchasing parts. You'll save time and money in the long run by doing so.

QA1 Measurement Table

Part Number	Compressed Height (inches)	Extended Height (inches)	Upper Mount	Lower Mount
403	10.13	14.00	Eyelet	Eyelet
505	08.75	13.50	Stud	T-Bar
506	10.39	15.35	Stud	Special
507	09.38	14.38	Stud	T-Bar
703	12.25	19.00	Stud	Eyelet
801	13.50	21.00	T-Bar	Eyelet
901	14.87	23.87	Eyelet	Eyelet
902	14.50	23.50	Stud	Eyelet
903	15.50	24.12	Stud	Eyelet

These drag-race-specific springs (from Moroso) are taller than factory coils to offer lift for a longer period while the car is launching. They work very well on drag cars and are highly recommended.

When selecting a shock you need your car's ride height measurement. Pick a shock in which the measurement is near the middle of the compressed and extended measurement. Most of the QA1 upper mounts can be changed to a different style.

Going to a coil-over setup gives you a better selection of springs and is usually just a few dollars more than a set of conventional springs and a good set of adjustable shocks of equal quality. With coil-overs, it is much easier (and safer) to change springs than with a taller conventional design coil.

That should be enough information to understand the workings of a double A-arm front suspensions car and point you in the right direction to make yours better, faster, and more consistent.

Safety Note

I vividly remember changing the front (conventional) taller coil springs in my Cutlass. I was using a spring compressor, but the compressor came loose, as did the spring. My hand was caught between the spring and the lower A-arm. I felt no pain, so I assumed my hand was crushed beyond use.

Luckily, my wife heard the noise of the coil spring releasing and came to see what had happened. Between the two of us (and some pry bars), we were able to pry the coil spring up just enough for me to pull my hand out without a scratch.

The 1/2-inch socket extension had jammed between the coil spring and the lower A-arm, relieving the pressure and protecting my hand from being completely smashed. That's why I couldn't feel any pain.

The moral to this story is, as always, to be very careful. Removing front coil springs is a dangerous job. These springs store more energy than most people think—holding up the front end of a car requires a lot of strength! Removing taller springs (no matter the weight capacity) is a very dangerous job, and should be done by a professional.

By the way, that is the last time I have ever changed my own front coil springs. I went to a coil-over setup after that. Coil-over setups are much less dangerous, since you can adjust the spring to release most (or all) of the spring tension before removal.

FRONT SUSPENSION: SINGLE A-ARM

The single A-arm suspension was designed by Earle S. MacPherson of General Motors in 1947, and is still widely used today. In contrast to a double A-arm suspension, a single A-arm suspension has the shock and coil spring combined into a single unit. This single unit uses less space allowing for more room, which is great for front-wheel-drive cars. The single arm design leaves ample room for the drive axles. Struts must provide support for the suspension with the springs, and the shock portion must also control the rate that weight is transferred during chassis movement.

Struts have to do more than their shock absorber counterparts, since all shocks have to do is control the rate that weight is transferred during chassis movement. Some of the more popular single A-arm-equipped muscle cars are the 1979–2011 Ford Mustangs and the 1982–1992 (third generation) GM Camaros and Firebirds.

The big difference between single A-arm and a double A-arm (single wishbone and double wishbone) front suspensions is that a double A-arm front suspension is adjustable for setting camber and caster with the upper A-arm, while a single A-arm front suspension (also referred to as MacPherson strut suspension) has the camber and caster fixed.

Single A-arm suspension, single-wishbone suspension, or MacPherson strut suspension are all accurate names for the parts discussed in this chapter. I refer to them throughout this book as single A-arm suspensions. Most of them have the A-arm on the bottom with a fixed top-mount for the strut (shock and spring unit). As discussed in Chapter 6, A-arms can be rather flat and triangular shaped. Since they are not part of the frame itself, but attach to the main frame, they are still considered a subframe. The end of the "A" with

Post-1979 Ford Mustangs (and all other Fox-chassis Ford vehicles) used a MacPherson-strut front suspension with great success. They are very popular drag cars due to their light weight and rear-wheel-drive design. (Photo by Eric McCellan)

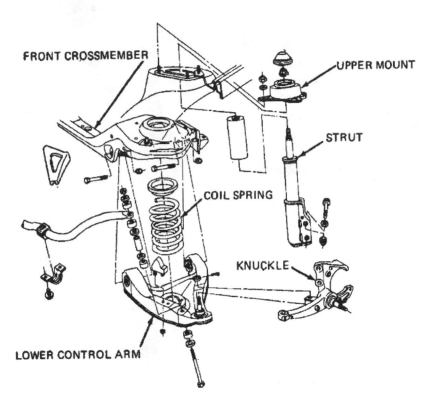

FRONT CROSSMEMBER

UPPER MOUNT

STRUT

COIL SPRING

KNUCKLE

LOWER CONTROL ARM

Here's an exploded view of a typical MacPherson strut front suspension design. This single-wishbone style is common in more modern cars, as it works well, has minimal components, and saves both weight and space when compared to double-wishbone designs.

two legs attaches to the frame and pivots, while the pointed end of the "A" attaches to the steering knuckle and pivots on a ball joint.

Alignment

With camber and caster being fixed and not adjustable, the only real alignment to be made is toe in or out (see page 44). However, years of running hard into curbs or big potholes or dropping hard from big wheel stands, the camber and caster can also become out of adjustment.

Toe is changed by turning the threaded sleeves connecting the tie rod ends making the tie rod ends farther apart or closer together. If the tie rod ends are on the front side of the steering knuckles (ball joints) then threading the tie rod longer creates

toe-out just as threading the tie rod ends shorter creates toe-in. If the tie rod ends are on the rear side of the steering knuckles (ball joints), the opposite actions must be taken.

Camber relates to the wheels being perpendicular or straight up and down. Significant suspension modifications like raising, lowering, or dropped spindles may require camber adjustments.

On drag-race-only cars, take a couple photos of the car from the side: one under full acceleration and the other near the far end of the racetrack before the finish line. Then, when the car is on the alignment rack you can reproduce the same stance and set the camber to near 0. Although this can give you a near-optimal camber setting for acceleration, it may not be the best setting

for tire wear. Since a strip-only car isn't going to see a lot of miles, it should be close enough not to wear the front tires unusually.

Caster deals with the spindle location governed by the upper and lower ball joints.

It is important to ensure that the caster is the same on both sides of a drag race car to remove the car's tendency to pull to one side on a flat surface making it harder to steer in a straight line. This can also cause scrubbing of the front tires resulting in poorer acceleration and in turn increased ETs.

Replacement Struts

Since camber and caster are fixed in single A-arm suspensions, other suspension changes need to be made to allow movement to correct camber and caster. The replacement struts (which have two lower bolts holding the strut to the spindle) may have the top hole elongated on some models. With the bottom hole in a fixed location, it can be used as a pivot to allow the top part of the strut to be tipped in or out. Tipping the strut in creates negative camber, while tipping the strut out creates positive camber.

If replacement struts are not available, the upper strut-mounting bolt holes can be slotted left to right, again allowing the strut to be tipped in or out. The same hole modifications can be made in different directions or just enlarged to adjust caster. If you take your street car with a single A-arm front suspension to an alignment shop they will probably correct camber and/or caster issues with this method.

Camber and Caster Plates

For racing cars with a different weight engine, a modified chassis

Using adjustable camber plates (such as these QA1 units) is the way additional camber can be dialed into MacPherson-strut-equipped cars once they've been lowered beyond the capability of the factory settings. These plates are easy to install and offer racers the adjustability they require.

stance, or higher horsepower, there is a better solution. Many companies make adjustable camber and caster plates for highly modified cars to be used as the top mount for the struts. Some of these adjustable caster and camber plates are designed to be welded in and some simply bolt into place. Do your homework and get the best parts for your particular application not only now, but for more modifications in the future.

Camber Kit

A way to adjust camber without slotting the strut mounting holes or using an adjustable plate is to use a camber kit. It consists of smaller-diameter bolts with an eccentric washer installed in place of one of the strut/spindle mount bolts. Since the diameter of the bolt is smaller, you can move the strut in or out due to the extra space created by the smaller bolt. These kits are commonly used on street-based cars since they install easily with no grinding needed. They are not advisable for a high-performance application due to the smaller-diameter bolt being weaker.

Sway Bars

On cars equipped with sway bars, it may be possible to remove them and see some gain in dragstrip performance. However, if that sway bar is used to help locate the lower control arm (as it is on some single A-arm suspension designs) it should remain in place. Research your particular application to see if this is the case. Most performance-oriented single A-arm independent suspension cars have sway bars (on the front to give additional handling stability).

Aftermarket Struts

Another drag race specific performance improvement is to replace the factory struts. As mentioned earlier, each side of the car utilizes a strut (shock absorber and coil spring kit) to absorb vibrations and bumps. Good-quality struts are very important for today's higher-horsepower cars. The front suspension in these cars as delivered from the factory works fairly well up to 300 hp. Cars at this horsepower level don't need a lot of suspension work to make the tires hook. If your car's horsepower is approaching this level, or you just want to be more consistent and improve the car's handling, there are several companies that offer front strut performance packages. You can easily start with a pair of single-adjustable struts, race-adjustable struts, or double-adjustable struts, then add the right components and get the right package for your needs.

Once your car's horsepower level goes beyond 300 I strongly suggest increasing the quality of the

Here is a QA1 single-adjustable replacement strut for Mustangs. Like other QA1 shock absorbers, the single knob at the bottom of the strut adjusts both compression and rebound stiffness.

QA1's double-adjustable strut offers independent adjustment of compression and rebound, just like its shock absorbers. The benefits are the same, too. These are also available for later-model (1983-newer) GM F-Bodies (Camaros and Firebirds) equipped with strut-type front suspensions.

With the spring in place this is what the complete QA1 strut looks like. It replaces the factory unit completely and offers ride-height adjustment by turning the collars on the threaded portion of the strut, thus raising or lowering the spring.

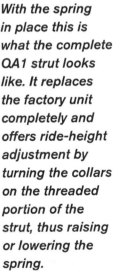

The double-adjustable strut/spring combination is seen here. You can spot the set screw through the collar that locks the spring height adjuster in place.

struts. You want to be able to adjust how quickly the front of the car comes up. At this horsepower level it probably doesn't come up high enough to be concerned about how quickly it comes down. Turning the knob in a counterclockwise direction creates a stiffer strut setting, allowing a quicker rise in the front of the car. Turning the knob in a clockwise direction creates a softer strut setting and a slower rise in the front of the car.

For a strip-only car, or one that gets very minimal street use, QA1 has an "R" (race) series single-adjustable strut. These have 18 valve settings but are much softer on extension (rebound) for better weight transfer (pitch rotation). These softer settings are great for the strip but not a good idea for street driving. Using these struts on a very rough or wavy road can cause unwanted actions from the cars suspension.

With adjustable struts, it's best to start near the middle. If your car needs more front-end lift (pitch rotation) then a softer setting may be needed. If your car's front end is raising too much, a firmer setting is needed.

For drag-race-only application, always run the lightest-weight spring that holds your car at the desired ride height to get the best weight transfer (pitch rotation) possible. Using a lighter-weight spring than factory causes the spring to collapse farther than normal. You therefore need a taller spring to keep the front end at normal ride height. With a lighter-weight spring compressed farther, the spring has stored energy and causes the front of the car to lift quicker and farther during acceleration and weight transfer (pitch rotation).

As explained in Chapter 10, knowing the car's total weight and the percentages of that weight bias from front to rear is critical. If you need some final chassis adjustments, such as when scaling the car and setting chassis preload, the QA1 strut bodies are threaded so the spring base can be adjusted up or down as needed taking the car's chassis up or down with it.

Bracing

Another improvement is to install a strut tower brace. In a strut-equipped car, the top of the strut is mounted into the tower. These towers are almost as high as the top of the front fender and are made from welded stamped-steel parts. Due to their height and the stress they are put through, the towers can flex up to 1/4-inch—there goes all the front-end settings you worked so hard to obtain. Steeda makes strut-tower braces. I like Steeda products because they're fabricated from chrome-moly material and serve to strengthen the front of a car. This helps to eliminate suspension flex and cowl shake while improving steering response and handling. Steeda products have extra clearance for popular aftermarket intakes and superchargers, making them a perfect upgrade. So if your car has a strut-type suspension and doesn't have a strut-tower brace, I highly recommend getting one.

With race cars no longer having stock suspension and/or different tire diameters than stock, or even different tire diameters front and rear, it is very important to look at proper strut ride-height. The last thing you need in any suspension is to have the strut bottom out in either direction. Similar to the shock absorber measurements outlined in sidebar "Proper Shock Length is Critical" on page 13, it's wise to remove the strut and measure the compressed and extended dimensions of the front suspension before purchasing aftermarket struts. This way you know that the strut has

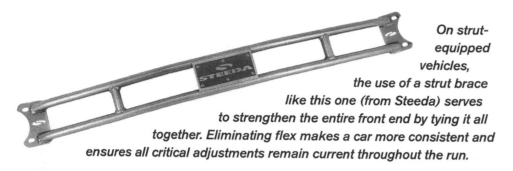

On strut-equipped vehicles, the use of a strut brace like this one (from Steeda) serves to strengthen the entire front end by tying it all together. Eliminating flex makes a car more consistent and ensures all critical adjustments remain current throughout the run.

adequate travel length to allow the suspension to fully compress and extend as it's designed to. Should a strut bottom out, the suspension's movement would suddenly ceases and maybe even begins to travel in the opposite direction. The impact this motion has upon the suspension can be very dangerous to the driver. Avoid this by researching the strut's travel requirements beforehand.

Coil-Overs, Struts, Springs, K-Members

As with all drag race cars a single A-arm or strut car benefits from narrower tires in the front. If you have a race-only car you may choose to run Moroso front tires (not DOT-approved tires). They are lighter in weight than a DOT-approved street tire and are for race-only usage. If you have a dual-purpose car that is street driven you need a tire that is DOT approved for street use, such as Mickey Thompson front tires. Either of these tires have what is referred to as a crowned tread. Having less tread on the ground with the crowned tread creates less rolling resistance and faster ETs but at a great sacrifice to cornering capabilities.

As with double A-arm cars, strut cars need taller and lighter weight front springs (trick springs), which contain "stored energy" from being lighter in weight (smaller wire diam-

eter) and yet still maintain ride height (by being taller). As the car begins to raise in the front with the lighter weight spring, the car lifts farther and quicker as weight is transferred than the stock factory springs.

Moroso makes a line of "trick springs" that bolt in with no modifications necessary (sometimes you may need to trim them for a more desired ride height but only after the car has set for a few days). These springs (PN 47240) fit the 1993 to 2002 Camaro and Firebird. They are rated for 1,500 to 1,700 pounds of front end weight. This is a 275-pound-per-inch spring. Moroso also makes "trick springs" for the 1979 to 2004 Ford Mustang. The Mustang version (PN 47220) is a 250-pounds-per-inch spring and rated for 1,750 to 1,900 pounds of front end weight.

These lighter weight and stronger tubular upper A-arms by AJE are for the 1979–2004 Mustang.

Moroso makes front struts for the 1982 to 1992 GM F-Bodies (Camaros and Firebirds) as well as the 1979 to 1993 Mustang. In a 50/50 standard-ratio strut there is as much resistance to the compression of the strut as to the extension of the strut. With these Moroso 90/10 struts there is only 10-percent resistance on the extension side to allow the car to raise quicker and farther for maximum weight transfer. The compression side has 90-percent resistance to help the front of the car from coming down too quick and too hard. Coming down too hard can cause a bouncing effect in the front of the car lifting the front wheels off the ground again and again. This unwanted repeated movement unloads the rear tires and then loads them again, as many times as the car bounces. For improved top end handling the chassis needs to come down slowly and return to the correct ride height.

K-Member Swaps

At the far end of the spectrum, toward the race-only part, lie the K-frame swaps. These upgrades are readily available for all the popular single A-arm performance cars like third- and fourth-gen GM F-Bodies (Camaro/Firebird), Fox-Bodied Fords, and all SN95 and newer Mustangs.

The upgrade consists of removing the factory K-member that ties the left and right front subframe together and replacing it with a tubular aftermarket unit. These are typically a bit stronger than the factory parts they replace, but they are notoriously lighter as well. The installations vary as widely as the manufacturers that make the parts.

For example, the Spohn Performance replacement K-member for

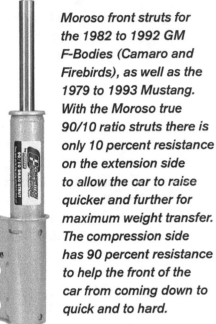

Moroso front struts for the 1982 to 1992 GM F-Bodies (Camaro and Firebirds), as well as the 1979 to 1993 Mustang. With the Moroso true 90/10 ratio struts there is only 10 percent resistance on the extension side to allow the car to raise quicker and further for maximum weight transfer. The compression side has 90 percent resistance to help the front of the car from coming down to quick and to hard.

QA1 makes an aftermarket K-member for the 1979–1993 and 1994–2004 Mustang which is stronger, lighter, and has improved geometry than the original factory piece.

Anthony Jones Engineering struts are adjustable for installed height, ride height and camber angle. Ford has at least five different spindles for the 1979–2004 Mustangs. These struts have different camber angles, different spindles, different spindle height, different steering arm locations, different ball joint attachment (Boss thickness), and different strut mounting. The new strut assemblies can be used on any 1979–2004 Mustang.

third-gen GM F-Bodies (1993–1997 Camaro/Firebird) is smaller, lighter, and significantly stronger than the stamped steel factory part it replaces. This particular K-member is recommended by the manufacturer for use in road racing and drag racing vehicles. Spohn also claims that vehicles equipped with their K-member upgrade are perfectly safe for street driving. The smaller dimensions of the overall tubular K-member package offer greater access and clearance under the car for things like exhaust headers, turbocharger system plumbing, aftermarket oil pans, etc.

This particular K-member is designed to be compatible with all other factory parts, like the motor mounts, steering rack, and front suspension arms. While you'd expect the front suspension components to

have been upgraded by the time an enthusiast is ready to upgrade something as serious as the K-member, it's good to know all the factory stuff still bolts up and functions just fine with this aftermarket K-member in place. Additionally, Spohn offers an upgrade steering rack for this K-member as well. It's a popular Pinto rack, and is a manual-steering unit. This sheds even more precious weight off the front end of the car, once installed.

It's also important to know that not all aftermarket K-member kits are

completely comfortable in a street environment. For instance, Racecraft Inc. also makes a K-member for 1982–1992 GM F-Bodies. This one, however, is specifically designed for drag racing cars. It offers the kind of clearance you hope for in a tubular K-member, so things like big-tube headers have plenty of room. It weighs only 21.7 pounds (when equipped with Pinto rack-and-pinion steering mounts) compared to the factory unit it replaces, which weighs 44.8 pounds. That's a savings of 23.1 pounds off the nose of the car! But, when you equip it with Racecraft's own 2-inch-drop spindle, you must commit to using Racecraft's Pinto rack-and-pinion kit and tapered-pin bumpsteer kit; and you really should upgrade to their Grade 8 hardware kit too.

It's a pretty major investment of both time and money to upgrade to an aftermarket K-member like these, but when you get to this level of performance, it's all justifiable.

Naturally, the Ford Fox body and Mustang components require similar effort for similar benefits. Spohn also has them, and other manufacturers (like UPR Products) have a complete line of replacement K-members for Mustangs dating back to 1979. These are also touted as being tough enough for daily driver use on the street.

AJE Suspension has brought a cutting-edge design to the market that has changed the way we look at front suspensions with K-members that are lighter, stronger, and that have more header clearance than the factory K-member provides. The AJE K-member's unique design provides engine mounts that mount any engine. This mounting system is used on various vehicles in addition to the 1979 to 2004 Mustang for which it was originally designed.

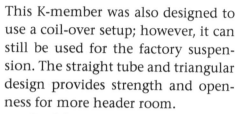

Replacement K-members from Anthony Jones Engineering are lighter in weight, stronger, have improved geometry, and are a bolt-in swap. The unique design provides engine mounts that mount any engine.

The front K-member from RaceCraft Inc fits 1982–1992 Camaro/Firebird Is made from TIG-welded 4130 chrome-moly. This Pinto rack-and-pinion drag race K-member is the industry standard when it comes to fit, finish, and design. This front hoop-style K-member provides maximum header clearance to fit larger exhaust systems. This K-member is a good choice for weight conscious 7- to 12-second factory suspension race cars.

This K-member was also designed to use a coil-over setup; however, it can still be used for the factory suspension. The straight tube and triangular design provides strength and openness for more header room.

Ford has had at least six different K-members for the 1979 to 2004 Mustang to be able to mount different engines, different rack locations, and different anti-dive angles. AJE has taken all of these into account when designing their latest K-member and front suspension package. The new struts are adjustable for installed height, ride height, and camber angle. They have different camber angles, different spindles, different spindle heights, different steering arm locations, different ball joint attachments (Boss thickness), and different strut mounting. The AJE new strut assemblies can be used on any 1979 to 2004 Mustang.

AJE's K-member lets you mount any engine including a twin turbocharged big-block that can produce ETs in the low-6-second range in the quarter-mile, plus speeds of more than 230 mph. When mounting different engines, oil pan–to-rack clearance becomes an issue. So being able to mount the rack in a factory location, 1 inch lower, or even changing to a 1971 Pinto-style

rack can be a big adventure for the oil pan clearance! This K-member lets you do that but it also allows you to mount a factory engine, factory springs, factory A-arms, and factory racks!

AJE has designed a factory replacement tubular A-arm that lets you retain the coil springs. However, the coil-over kit, tubular A-arms, and K-member can remove up to 70 pounds from the front end. The coil-over kit also allows ride height adjustments, making it one of the best options for your Mustang.

Coil-overs let you select the best spring rate for your intended use. When going from factory springs to coil-overs the spring rate needs to change. The factory rates are higher. Looking at the spring location in the factory A-arms, you need to factor in the leverage ratio of about 2:1 and the coil-over is closer to a 1:1 ratio. This means that a coil-over setup used for road racing needs to be in the 300- to 400-pound range. A daily driver needs 150- to 200-pound rates. A drag race car with around 500 hp and weighing 3,000 pounds or less could use 125- to 150-pound springs. A driver wanting a good ride and good handling also could use a variable-rate spring in the 175- to 350-pound range.

AJE's new strut assemblies provide new options. Some Mustang owners want to lower the ride height of their car. With a stock setup you have to trim coils off the springs or go to a softer rate making it more likely to bottom-out the strut. With the new AJE struts you can lower the body of the strut in 1/2-inch increments to keep this from happening.

Another modification Mustang owners like is to use the later SN95 spindles on a Fox Mustang. Bigger and better brakes along with more drop in the spindle are the pluses. The SN95 spindle has more camber angle and the A-arm is longer. Using SN95 A-arms moves the wheels out about 1 inch.

When using Fox A-arms with SN95 spindles, the strut doesn't match up to the attachment point in the strut tower, making the camber wrong. AJE's new struts have an adjustable-camber key that can be used in a factory location, or add 3 of camber angle or decrease 3 of camber angle. For drag racing the Fox spindles can provide lighter brakes and are able to pull the tires under the car for a lower ride height. The AJE struts come with adjustable valving so whether you are drag racing, road racing, or just taking a drive, AJE has the front suspension you need.

FRONT SUSPENSION: TORSION BARS

A torsion bar is a long round spring steel bar that resists twisting and returns to its original position after being twisted, thus providing a spring action for the car. It is a form of a weight-bearing spring. Torsion-bar suspension systems were used in most Chrysler vehicles of the 1950s, 1960s, and 1970s, Cadillac Eldorado, Oldsmobile Toronado, Packard, and more. They are currently used in trucks and SUVs from Ford, General Motors, and Dodge. Although all of these torsion-bar systems operate basically in the same manner, this book concentrates on the Chrysler-built cars as they are still popular on most drag strips around the country.

Chrysler had three main passenger car platforms called A, B, and E. The A-Body torsion bars were 35.7 inches long, while the B- and E-Body bars were 41 inches long. For all three bodies, the hex end measured 1¼ inches. Therefore any bar with the same length could be swapped into another car regardless of diameter.

Chrysler A-Body cars with 35.7-inch-long torsion bars include:

1960–1976 Plymouth Valiant
1963–1976 Dodge Dart
1964–1969 Plymouth Barracuda
1971–1976 Plymouth Scamp
1970–1976 Plymouth Duster
1961–1962 Dodge Lancer
1971–1972 Dodge Demon

Chrysler B-Body cars with 41-inch-long torsion bars include:

1962 Dodge Dart
1962–1964 Dodge Polara
1962–1964 Plymouth Fury
1962–1964 Plymouth Savoy
1962–1970 Plymouth Belvedere
1963–1964 Dodge 330
1963–1964 Dodge 440
1965–1974 Plymouth Satellite
1965–1976 Dodge Coronet
1966–1978 Dodge Charger
1967–1971 Plymouth GTX
1968–1975 Plymouth Road Runner
1975–1978 Plymouth Fury

This Hemi-powered 1968 Barracuda runs in the ultra-competitive Super Stock Automatic class. It's launching perfectly, with the front end nice and level. This shows all the power hitting the rear tires, and none being used to twist the chassis.

This 1964 Dodge is also Hemi-powered, and was photographed at the 1969 NHRA World Finals in Dallas, Texas. The torsion-bar-equipped Mopars work just fine at the drag strip, as many years of success in the Stock classes will attest.

1975–1979 Chrysler Cordoba
1977–1978 Dodge Monaco
1978–1979 Dodge Magnum
1979 Chrysler 300

Chrysler E-Body cars with 41-inch long torsion bars include:

1970–1974 Dodge Challenger
1970–1974 Plymouth Barracuda

Basic Design

The torsion-bar system from a 1972 Dodge Demon consists of two round steel bars (one left and one right) with a 1¼-inch hex on both ends measuring 35.7 inches long. The torsion bars run from the floorpan crossmember to the front lower suspension arms. The rear mount of the torsion bar is inserted into a six-sided socket built into the floorpan crossmember, which is perpendicular to the torsion bar. The front mount of the torsion bar is a six-sided socket built into a lever and attached inside the lower suspension arm, also perpendicular to the torsion bar. The lever in the lower suspension arm has an adjuster that can apply more or less pressure (preload) on the torsion bar.

He may have left a little early (note the red light) but he left strong! This 1972 Dodge Demon belongs to Caffey Broadus and was seen at the National Muscle Car Association (NMCA) Finals in Memphis, Tennessee, in 2009.

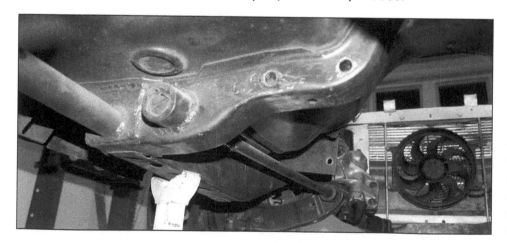

A torsion bar is simply another kind of spring. Here we see a basic torsion bar setup under another Dodge Demon. The reshaped end fits into the chassis, and the lower control arm fits onto the other end.

The rear (chassis) torsion bar mount consists of a basic hex shape. The bar fits into the hex and is secured with a simple clip.

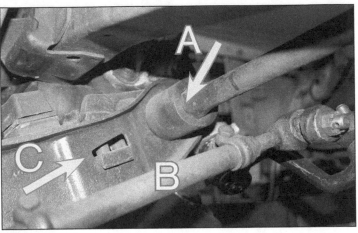

The front of the bar has another hex shape (A), which fits into the lower control arm. You can see the tie rods behind the control arm (B), and the adjuster bolt (C) threads through the small window in the arm itself.

The adjuster bolt is seen at the bottom on the left-hand side of the control arm. This sets the preload on the arm, and the vehicle can be raised or lowered by simply tightening or loosening this bolt.

Performance Upgrades

Torsion bar front suspension systems as used in all Chrysler, Plymouth, and Dodge vehicles (beginning in 1957 and lasting through 1979), are perhaps the easiest suspension systems to modify that were available as original equipment. Torsion-bar front suspensions are very durable and offer easy adjustment of ride height, regardless of age. The torsion-bar suspension system easily converts the front of the car from a streetable setup to a drag-race setup by adjusting or replacing the torsion bars with bars of a different diameter (strength) and adding race-quality single-adjustable or double-adjustable shocks under the front. Once the right torsion bars have been installed, it is very important to have a good set of quality shocks to control the spring rate.

Torsion bars can easily be swapped for bars with a lighter spring rate. Just as you can replace front springs in a GM- or Ford-built car with lighter-rated and taller "trick" springs to create stored energy (allowing the front to raise more readily), you can go to a smaller-diameter torsion bar that produces the same effect. Then the torsion bar can be adjusted with the lower suspension arm adjustment bolt to give the desired ride height, just as you do by using taller or shorter springs with the same weight rating (pounds per inch). Depending upon how you set the adjuster you can add or take away preload, raise or lower the car, and allow more or less weight transfer upon acceleration. Instead of changing to a different spring, the preload is adjusted by forcing rotational twist of the torsion bar. Screwing the bolt in farther puts more pressure (preload) on the torsion bar and unscrewing the bolt applies less pressure (preload) on the torsion bar.

More preload with smaller-diameter torsion bars acts the same as a GM or Ford car with lighter-weight taller springs, which also give the cars stored energy to lift it faster and harder than it previously did. Changing to a torsion bar of lighter weight or smaller diameter requires the adjuster to be screwed in farther, creating even more preload.

This disassembled lower control arm shows how all the pieces fit together and make the torsion bar system work. To make this a little easier to understand, pictured is a disassembled suspension arm showing the three parts that help the torsion bar do its job. Shown is the lever that the torsion bar slides into, the bolt with the rounded end that adjusts the lever (preload), and the nut that is threaded so the bolt may be adjusted up or down (more or less preload), which applies the twist on the suspension arm.

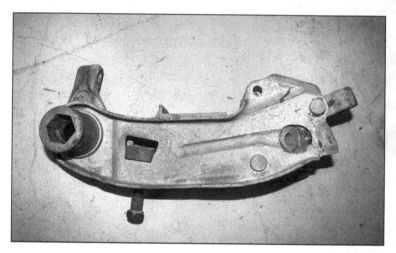

Shown is a suspension arm that is fully assembled with the lever still in the air, ready to rotate onto the bolt. You can see the cup that the adjuster bolt seats into.

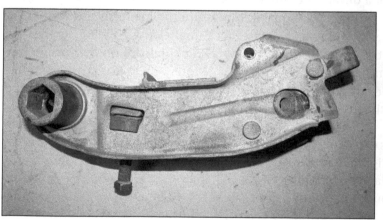

This fully assembled torsion bar lower control arm is ready to be put back into service. When the wheel hits a bump, the lower suspension arm is forced upward. This action pivots and twists the torsion bar. The torsion bar's resistance to the twist holds the wheel on the road just as a conventional coil spring does. This style of suspension system takes up less space, offering a weight-savings advantage. Additionally, there is more room under the vehicle, allowing the engine to be placed lower in the chassis, offering a lower and safer center of gravity. The lower suspension features a single arm (not triangulated) which has a diagonally mounted strut rod attached to it that reinforces and positions the arm and front wheel and is also attached to the front subframe.

Naturally, every car will respond differently. The main idea here is to know that the parts exist and that different shock and torsion bar combinations are available to fine-tune your vehicle's launch characteristics. Your car's torque, horsepower, weight, tire size, and gearing has different needs than another similar car with different specifications.

Although many diameter torsion bars are available, the following are recommended as a starting point for maximum weight transfer during hard acceleration.

Drag Tuning

There is no "one size fits all" setup, nor are there enough pages here to give exact settings for every combination. The following information will help to get you started.

Torsion bars used for drag racing should be of as small a diameter as possible for more weight transfer (pitch rotation), yet strong enough to support the front of the car under all conditions. To plant the rear tires as hard as possible when launching a car with a factory-style suspension, it is necessary to get as much weight transfer (pitch rotation) as possible and to do so as quickly as possible.

Upper Control Arm

Lower Control Arm

Torsion Bar

Pivot Point

This graphic shows how the torsion bar provides spring pressure for the front suspension. The bar is twisted when the vehicle encounters a bump in the road, and then it forces the wheel/tire assembly back down to compensate.

The front suspension must be held in position, and this diagonally mounted strut rod does the job. These do wear and must be checked regularly to ensure ride quality.

This is what the back end of the strut rod looks like. The strut rods are firmly mounted into the chassis.

You don't want the rear tires to start moving any distance before the weight starts to transfer. Smaller-diameter bars are lighter in strength and weight, and therefore respond quicker than the heavier bars they replace.

For example, 100 pounds taken off a smaller-diameter torsion bar raises the front of the car farther and quicker than 100 pounds taken off a larger-diameter torsion bar. Care must be used when using smaller-diameter torsion bars on the street. Smaller-diameter torsion bars may not be sufficient to control the car in a street-driving situation, even if they acheive what is needed for the drag strip. Traveling down a rough, uneven road surface using smaller-diameter torsion bars can get your car bouncing up and down uncontrollably, like a boat going over rough waves. Be honest with yourself regarding your vehicle's true intended purpose, and choose the best-possible bar for your application.

Too much weight transfer (pitch rotation) makes the car slower in 60-foot clockings. During pitch rotation, the front bumper of the car rotates in a circle using the rear tires as the axis. Therefore, as the front bumper raises, it is actually moving in an upward and rearward direction. The more pitch rotation and rearward movement of the front of the car, the more torque the engine needs to move the car forward the same distance in the same amount of time.

For the A-Body with 35.7-inch-long bars:

- .890-inch diameter for heavy big-block applications with partial street use
- .870-inch diameter for small-block applications with partial street use
- .810-inch diameter for six-cylinder or all-out drag race V-8 applications with no street use

For the B- and E-Body with 41-inch-long bars:

- .960-inch diameter for heavy big-block applications with partial street use
- .920-inch diameter for small-block applications with partial street use
- .840-inch diameter for six-cylinder or all-out drag race V-8 applications with no street use

Although this is also addressed in Chapter 2, it needs to be mentioned here, too. If you are running rear leaf springs that have more arch on the passenger's side for the purpose of preload (such as the Chrysler Super Stock springs), you need to raise the driver-side front with the torsion bar adjuster to lower the passenger-side rear corner to level the car (side-to-side). This preload on the right rear tire helps control torque roll in the chassis.

Shock Absorbers

The shocks must be upgraded to an adjustable race-designed unit that has the ability to be loosened or tightened as your car demands. Not all tracks are the same, nor is one track the same from week to week. A good set of adjustable racing shocks gives you the ability to adjust your suspension to maximize your car's performance. Remember, a good-hooking car is more consistent and the driver has a better chance to win the race with the confidence that the car is working right. A good-hooking car with everything else running properly allows confidence and accuracy when predicting ETs.

Many manufacturers offer a good choice of quality adjustable shocks with aluminum bodies for the A-, B-, and E-Body cars. The QA1 PN TC-1538-P is a single-adjustable shock that I recommend for mild street use and some drag racing with less than 450 hp. The knob has 12 valving options to adjust both compression and rebound (extension) simultaneously, allowing suspension control in one easy-to-reach knob. For drag race only applications with 450 to 600 hp, I suggest the QA1 PN RC-1538-P, which is similar to the TC-1538-P except that it comes with a fixed firm compression and 12 valving options to adjust rebound (extension) only. For cars with 600 hp or more, or the racer who wants to be able to fine-tune the suspension for every tenth of a second possible, I suggest the double-adjustable QA1 PN DTC-1538-P. It is adjustable independently in both compression and rebound (extension). This shock has 24 different positions on each knob for a total of 576 valving options. The knobs are clearly labeled. The "+" direction firms the action while the "-" direction softens it.

A good starting point for any adjustable shock is in the middle of the settings. If your car is lifting too high in the front, the front shocks need to be set to a stiffer setting on extension. You may also need to

Here's a close-up look at the torsion bar adjuster bolt. This is typical for all Chrysler vehicles made between 1957 and 1980.

The Chrysler A-Bodies (Dodge Dart/Plymouth Valiant) were lightweight and had plenty of room for both small-block and big-block V-8s. This Caffey Broadus example is launching perfectly. Again, note the level front end, raising about a foot off the ground.

add travel limiters to shorten the travel before the front tires leave the pavement. This greatly reduces the amount of travel before the front tires lift, thus slowing the pitch rotation and making it harder to jerk the front tires as high off the ground. If your car needs more weight transfer, use a looser extension setting and trim (or remove) the upper control arm bump stops for maximum front suspension travel.

If your race car is coming down hard after the launch and bouncing, the front shocks need to be stiffer on compression so the car doesn't hit the pavement as hard. Ideally the front of your car will come down as softly as it rose. How high your car raises in the front depends not only upon your suspension, but also upon how much torque your combination makes and at what RPM. The proper match of the torque converter (in automatic-transmission-equipped cars), camshaft, and intake within your peak torque RPM range also makes a huge difference in how the car reacts at the starting line upon

launch. Obviously, this has a lot more to do with engine design than with suspension, but it does impact how a car launches. A well-matched power package is a big part of finding success at the drag strip.

Weight Loss

A lot of drag racing success comes down to power and weight. Finding more power is one thing, but losing weight is another subject altogether. Did you know that cars have two types of weight (sprung and unsprung)? Unsprung weight is any weight below the springs that supports the chassis. Unsprung weight is considered dead weight and cannot be taken advantage of during pitch rotation (weight transfer). The only way to use unsprung weight to your advantage is to reduce it. For example, replacing steel wheels with lighter-weight aluminum versions. Front wheels and tires can also be reduced in diameter and width for greatly reduced unsprung weight. Be sure to check the weight of new wheels and tires

before purchasing them. I have seen aluminum wheels that were thicker and actually weighed as much as the steel wheels they were replacing. Rear slicks can be run without tubes to also reduce weight but at a reduction in sidewall stiffness.

In conrast, sprung weight can be used in pitch rotation (weight transfer) to add more weight over the rear axle to plant the rear tires harder. This is where the suspension needs to be fine-tuned to allow the front of the car to go up high enough to transfer the right amount of weight to the rear tires so the car hooks as well as possible.

Another way to take advantage of weight during launch is to remove as much of it as possible from the front of the car. If your car has to run a minimum weight for a particular class, any weight removed from the front of the car needs to be reinstalled in the back of the car. One good example is relocating the battery to the trunk. Safely using the lightest-possible components in the front of the car is always a good way to go to help your car accelerate more quickly. For instance, removing the inner fenders or adding an all-aluminum radiator, aluminum cylinder heads, aluminum intake manifold, fiberglass fenders and a fiberglass hood, all reduce the weight of the front of the car, allowing it to accelerate faster.

Also, lighter-weight front brakes could be used. Chuck Lofgren, Chrysler specialist and owner of Lofgren Auto Specialties, states that on his car, going from factory disc brakes to drum brakes saved close to 20 pounds per side (40 pounds total) in weight. Going to an aftermarket disc brake could save another 15 pounds per side (30 pounds total) in weight. (Lofgren

Auto Specialties makes and sells after-market suspension parts and builds engines, specializing in both early- and late-model Chrysler muscle cars.)

Last, but not the least important, are the alignment angles used to cor-rect bump steer or toe change due to front suspension travel. Achiev-ing 1½-degrees positive caster and 1/4-degree positive camber corrects the toe pattern to be within 1/8-inch total toe change throughout the sus-pension travel.

Subframe Connectors

Torsion-bar-equipped cars are made of a unibody construction, which means they don't have con-tinuous frame rails from the front of the car to the rear of the car. The frame and body are integrated as a single unit. Structural integrity is designed into the vehicle's floor-pan. For racing, install subframe connectors to tie the front and rear subframes together. This stiffens the car and helps reduce body twist, making the car respond better to racing conditions.

These handy prefabricated con-nector packages let you tie the front and rear subframe longitudi-nally and are available for all A-, B-, or E-Body drag cars. Packages include two connectors, brackets, and the necessary mounting hardware. Frame connectors can be bolted in or welded in depending on individual preference. Mancini Racing has more than 45 years of drag racing experi-ence and has developed a line of rac-ing parts for the front or rear of your Chrysler-based race car.

Bars and Cages

Another frame modification you can make is to add a roll bar or roll cage. For bracket racing, current NHRA rules dictate that a roll bar is mandatory in all cars running 11.00 to 11.49 seconds in the quarter-mile (7.00 to 7.35 seconds in the eighth-mile) and all convertibles running 11.00 to 13.49 seconds in the quar-ter-mile (7.00 to 8.25 seconds in the eighth-mile). But they are permitted in all cars. In my opinion, they are necessary in all unibody cars, not only for safety but for helping elimi-nate body roll and flex. A well-built roll bar or cage can actually aid trac-tion. Energy that once twisted the body and chassis is now directed to the tires.

Current NHRA rules also dic-tate that a roll cage is mandatory

QA1's double-adjustable shock absorbers offer a wide range of settings to maximize weight transfer under virtually any drag car.

Similarly, QA1's single-adjustable shocks simultaneously increase compression and rebound. They are a bit more budget friendly.

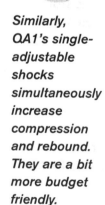

These subframe connectors from Mancini Racing tie the front and rear chassis subframes together to add strength and reduce flex. Most Chrysler cars of the muscle car era have subframes, and these are highly recommended for any that will be drag raced.

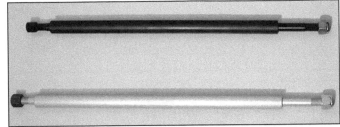

A wide selection of torsion bars are still available from Chrysler. Consult an expert (like Mancini Racing) to determine which bars are best for your particular applications.

in all cars running 10.99 seconds or quicker in the quarter-mile (6.99 seconds in the eighth-mile), or any car exceeding 135 mph. For full-bodied cars with unaltered firewalls, floors, and bodies from the firewall rearward with or without wheel tubs running quarter-mile times of 10.00 (eighth-mile 6.40) to 10.99 seconds (eighth-mile 6.99) a roll bar is permitted in place of a roll cage.

The actual rules are more detailed than this, so be sure to consult the current NHRA rule book or call NHRA technical support for the interpretations of the current rules.

Bushings

Front suspension arm bushings made of rubber were used in passenger cars for both ride and comfort. For racing, they should be replaced with polyurethane bushings for better suspension control. These give the car more stability, and as you make other suspension changes, the car responds better due to the lack of flex in the hard polyurethane as compared with the softer rubber.

Polyurethane bushing packages are available through Mancini Racing, as well as front strut bars to keep the front lower suspension arms in the proper place. Made of heavy-duty steel, these struts are a full 1 inch in diameter, which is 43 percent thicker than the original struts. Also,

for those who are weight conscious (remember, lighter means faster), they are available in aluminum which is CNC machined using 7075-T651 material and are .875 inch in diameter (compared with about .700 inch in diameter for the original steel struts). The aluminum weight is 36 percent as much as the equivalent amount of steel, so these struts are both stronger and lighter than the original components.

Tubular Arms

Mancini Racing carries a complete line of torsion bars and tubular upper front suspension arms. The upper arms are jig built, heli-arc welded, and powdercoated. They come with Moog balljoints and urethane inner bushings. Mancini engineers them with some extra positive caster for improved stability. A set of these arms dramatically improves the way your car drives. Mancini also offers stiffeners for your lower control arms with a lower-control-arm plate kit. These kits contain two steel plates and can be welded into any A-, B-, or E-Body lower control arm.

You should now have enough information to get the front of your torsion-bar-equipped car ready for the drag strip. While testing in time trials, focus on the 60-foot times to see if you are making positive or negative adjustments. Remember, one

sample 60-foot time is not enough to make any firm conclusions about the next adjustment. A minimum of two 60-foot times must be used. If they are not very similar, you have an issue that needs to be addressed before moving on to another adjustment. Otherwise, you are basing your last adjustment on inaccurate information.

Boxing stamped-steel control arms is a good idea. Here's a boxed Mopar lower front control arm, which shows that everyone understands the importance of minimizing flex and adding strength to these suspension components.

TIRES

Suspension and tire development have been the two greatest contributing factors in the ever-decreasing ETs of the sportsman racing categories. Yes, there are continually many new ways to build additional power too, but that power couldn't be used if there hadn't also been stronger and better parts made available. None of these results would have been achieved had it not been for the tires and suspensions that have been developed to handle the power. Drag racing suspensions and drag racing tires have gone hand-in-hand with the evolution of drag racing.

This is a recapped racing slick from Hurst Racing Tires. These represented the absolute cutting edge of racing technology in the early 1960s.

Just as with passenger car tires, several manufacturers specialize in racing tires. I have used just about all of them at some time over the years, including recapped cheater slicks from the 1960s, and don't have an issue with any of them. The biggest problem I see with racers is not recognizing the fact that when they switch to a different brand of tire they must follow that manufacturer's guidelines. Each tire maker specifies the type of tire needed, the method for breaking in the tire, and how to get the best-possible results at the track.

On the drag strip, mixing radials with bias-ply tires front to rear (not side-to-side) is allowable, but not recommended for the street. Drag racing is not considered a sustained duration of speed and therefore the poor handling characteristics you experience during normal street driving do not show.

Offset Axle Housings

Sometimes rear axles are not perfectly centered under the car when it's assembled at the factory, and you may need to run different wheel back spacing on each side if you don't take the time to center the axle yourself. Depending on how close the tires fit, this may prevent you from swapping tires side-to-side to clean the tread. You can run a wheel spacer on one side to create extra backspacing and still allow for the tires to be swapped side-to-side.

Be sure to check your local track's rulebook to determine the wheel stud lengths necessary when running aftermarket wheels and/or spacers (if legal).

Rubber Compounds

Racing tires come in many different hardness compounds. Since drag-racing tires have a softer compound than typical street tires, you would think that softer is better. This is not always true. Softer-compound tires are better for a lighter-weight vehicle, while a harder compound tire is better on heavier vehicles. If the compound is too hard on a lighter vehicle, it may reduce traction. If the compound is too soft on a heavier vehicle, it can cause premature wear.

I learned this the hard way in the early 1970s at an NHRA National meet. I was using a very soft compound tire on my 3,800-pound Cutlass, running the Stock Eliminator class. I wore out a set of Goodyear tires in one weekend! This was not Goodyear's fault, but mine. I learned a lot while experimenting for that ultimate goal of the best ET possible. It was an expensive experiment, but one never repeated. Be sure to follow the manufacturer's recommendations.

Your car's transmission also helps determine the compound of the tire needed. Drag tires are designed to either dead hook or have a controlled spin.

If you have a tire that dead hooks, you could get either tire shake or bog the motor when dumping the clutch. Since automatic-transmission cars have a torque converter and don't launch as violently as clutch-equipped cars, a dead-hook tire works best.

A high-horsepower car with a manual transmission needs a tire that has a controlled amount of spin.

Wheel Screws

If you are running soft compound tires, I suggest drilling the wheels for mounting screws to prevent the tire from turning on the wheel when hooking at the starting line. To install these, mount the tires and inflate them to 25 psi. Before drilling holes and installing the screws into the wheel, be sure they are not so long that they protrude through the tire bead and into the inside of the tire. Racing tires have an extra thick bead where the tire mounts to the wheel to accommodate the screws, and many manufacturers sell the proper-length wheel-mounting screws to accomplish this task without problem. Six to eight screws per side of a wheel is sufficient.

If you are running tubes and a tire spins on the wheel, it can cause the tire to pinch the tube. Whether you are running tubes or not this can not only throw the tire out of balance but also break the bead seal between the tire and the wheel.

If you are not sure if you need screws, you can use a piece of chalk or white shoe polish (common at the track for writing dial-in times on the window glass) to mark a straight line on both the wheel and the tire. When you check this line after making a pass, and it no longer lines up, the tire is slipping on the rim.

Tire Care

One important issue often overlooked is proper care of the tires. The following is a short list of suggestions and conventional wisdom concerning this topic.

Break-in and Rotation

Tires need to be broken in (or "seasoned"). Some tires (like Goodyear's racing tires) are directional until broken in (usually three to eight passes). Serial numbers on Goodyear rear tires must be mounted facing the driver's side of the car with one facing inboard and the other facing outboard. Goodyear front-tire serial numbers should face the passenger side of the car (also one in and one out). After any brand of rear tire is broken in, they should be rotated side-to-side as frequently as possible. Front tires should not be rotated.

Phoenix racing tires are directional according to the arrows on the sidewall until broken in, which usually takes about 15 passes. BF Goodrich's drag radials require a final curing process after the tires first hit the pavement. Hoosier and Mickey Thompson tires are not directional, but should be rotated as frequently as possible.

This is Mickey Thompson's current ET Street tire. They are DOT-legal and offer greater traction than the recapped race-only Hurst slick.

The reason some tires are directional has to deal with the way the seams mate together when the tire is built. Running directional tires in the wrong way can peel the tread off the tire.

Tires need to be rotated frequently because the tread can ball up as it wears. Running tires in the opposite direction gets rid of the balling and smooths out the tread once again. Trying to launch a car on a tire that has little rubber balls all over it is like trying to launch on marbles. If the tires are DOT approved, driving them on the street should also remove the rubber ball buildup.

I suggest rotating your tires every weekend. You will get better traction and a much extended tire life.

Storage

When storing your tires for the off-season, remove them from the car or at least jack up the car to get them off the ground. Drop the air pressure to about 5 psi and keep them out of direct sunlight.

Tires should not be stored around welding areas or high-voltage elec-

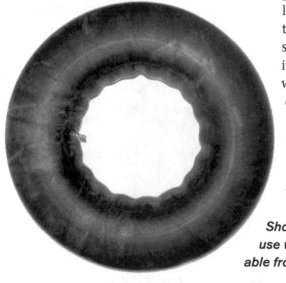

Shown is a natural rubber inner tube for use with racing slicks. These are available from Mickey Thompson.

tric motors. Keep them covered and avoid extreme cold or heat (including heat-generating electric motors, furnaces, air compressors, etc.).

Also, tires should not be allowed to freeze when wet.

Inner Tubes

Many racers feel that bias-ply drag racing slicks (wrinkle wall) should be run without inner tubes, since that creates a lighter weight mass to rotate. While that is correct, a couple other factors contribute to the decision whether to use a tube or not.

A heavy car that hits the tire hard upon launch might be better off with inner tubes to add strength and stability to the sidewalls, giving less wrap-up and therefore a quicker response time. Additionally, tires equipped with tubes don't leak air during the week between races. Radial drag racing tires already have a built-in liner and stiffer sidewalls, and therefore don't need tubes.

Air Pressure

Always run as much air as possible in your rear tires. The more pressure the better. More air creates less rolling resistance and makes the tire roll easier. With too little air pressure, the car tends to drive the wheel into the ground at the starting line, which could pinch the tube and/ or debead the tire as well as let the tire cup in the middle of the tread (thus creating two small footprints instead of one larger one).

Also, with too little air pressure, the car tends to sway at higher speeds

on the top end of the track. When experimenting with tire pressures, anytime I get that swaying effect, I know I am at least 2 to 4 pounds short of air pressure from what the tire wants, regardless of what is happening at the starting line.

Tread Depth

It is not uncommon for tires to lose grip while still having tread left. I have seen racers with slower cars run their tires (while not recommended) until the cords show, and not notice much reduction in ET. On the other hand I have had customers call needing technical help because their car had slowed down for no apparent reason. First, I ask if their speed has decreased (indicating horsepower level). If not, the next question is how old or how many runs they have on their rear tires. After eliminating other possibilities it becomes apparent that the tread may have worn away.

If you are losing traction and have sufficient tread left, unless you change your burnout method, it will probably happen again at about the same time as with the last set of tires. To increase tire life, do not overheat them (do the minimal burnout you need to get full traction, and no more), and when the tires get a grainy texture on the tread, reverse them to smooth them out again.

After each weekend of racing, I always use a tread depth indictor to check the tire's tread depth in about four places across the tread to be sure I have even wear. If it's not even, there may be a tire pressure issue. Too much wear on the outside edges indicate that the tires need more air. Too much wear in the middle indicates that the tires need less air. I am talking small changes of 1 to 2 pounds.

Inner-Tube Installation

Once you have made the decision to run inner tubes in your bias-ply drag racing slicks, always run natural rubber tubes. Here's the right way to install them so they don't twist or leak:

1. Fill the tube with air and check to ensure the stem has the correct side up before you install the tube into the tire. The wheels have the valve stem hole on the outside, and the tube must have its stem pointing in the same outward direction.
2. Liberally coat the inside of the tire and the outside of the tubes with baby powder. This helps prevent the wrinkle-wall action from pinching a hole into the tube, which will surely happen with regular passenger car tires.
3. Carefully load the tube inside the slick, being careful not to twist it. Work your way around the entire wheel until the tube is fully installed.

If you follow these simple tips, you should have no problems with inner tubes inside your drag slicks. The tubes should encounter no wear and should outlive the life of the slicks. If you feel a tube may be leaking, remove it, fill it with air, and submerge it under water. If you see bubbles, you've found the leak! Spraying the tube with a mix of soapy water is also an effective way to find leaks. If you see bubbles, you've found the source of the leak.

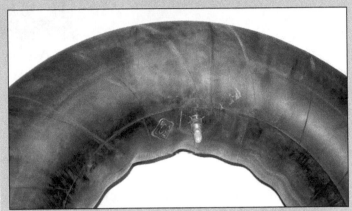

One of the features that separates Mickey Thompson inner tubes from the rest is the placement of the valvestem. Note that it's offset to the outside—this is designed to align with the offset hole in the wheel while keeping the tube centered on the rim.

When racing slicks wrinkle, they can pinch and puncture inner tubes. The natural rubber used by Mickey Thompson is capable of dealing with this kind of abuse.

Mounting Advice

About 24 hours before mounting DOT-approved street or drag-only tires without tubes, liberally coat the inside of the tire (particularly the inside sidewall) with dish soap. This creates a coating inside the tire to help prevent air leaks through the tire. It also allows the soap to dry in place so the moisture from mounting the tire (air and rim) doesn't wash soap off any part of the tire. By the way, I have had better luck with Palmolive brand dish soap than other brands.

Most tire shop air compressors have very high moisture content due to running almost constantly. By sure to take your own baby powder or dish soap in case the tire shop doesn't have any.

Always run as large a tire as possible, both height-wise and width-wise. For the best traction possible, a taller

After both tires produce steady smoke, stage the car as soon as possible to keep heat in the tires.

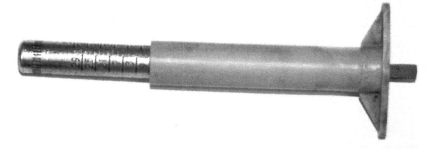

A typical tread depth gauge like this one is placed into the holes in the slick's tread to get an accurate reading. Consult the tire manufacturer to learn your tire's minimal safe depth.

Mickey Thompson's ET Drag tires are not DOT-approved and can be used for racing only. These slicks represent the best-possible drag racing tires available, and they work very well.

On DOT-approved treaded tires, use the tread depth gauge in the deepest portion of the tread. Check several places around the tires on both sides of the car to ensure they are wearing evenly.

and wider tire has a larger actual footprint on the pavement than a shorter, narrower tire. Go for the largest footprint possible unless you are running a low-horsepower engine in a heavy car, which (because of the weight and size of the larger tire) could actually slow down the car. If you have stock wheel wells, you may also have to measure the wheel backspacing clearance carefully before ordering custom wheels to get the largest tire possible into the limited space.

Most non-radial drag tires are suggested to be mounted with tubes. However, using the dish soap method I described it is possible to run a bias-ply drag tire without a tube. It's always a gamble as to if the dish soap will completely seal the sidewall 100 percent. The good side of not running tubes is weight savings. One pound of unsprung weight is equal to 8 pounds of sprung weight. Therefore, every 12 pounds of unsprung weight removed the car may gain .01 seconds in the quarter-mile. However, on heavy cars the additional sidewall stability from using a tube inside the drag tire may offset the ET lost from weight in traction gained.

Street Tire Comparison

I have had great success using Mickey Thompson (M/T) drag and street tires. If you are contemplating M/T ET Drag tires, ET Street tires, ET Drag Radials, or ET Street Radials, be sure to do your homework before making that purchase. You're safe with either the ET Drag or ET Drag Radial tires, as they are strictly drag race tires. Not all ET Street or ET Street Radials are 100 percent identical to their Drag counterparts. I recently had an opportunity to test a pair of ET Drag tires (29.5x10.5x15S)

Holly Springs Motorsports

RUN 83   04/30/11 5:16:41 PM
FOOTBRAKE   TT RD #1

LEFT:5867
000.00 ---- DIAL IN
0.5212 ---- REACTION
1.6059 ---- 60 FT
4.5662 ---- 330 FT
7.0478 ---- 1/8 ET
098.94 ---- 1/8 MPH

Holly Springs Motorsports

RUN 89   04/30/11 5:21:02 PM
FOOTBRAKE   TT RD #1

LEFT:5867
000.00 ---- DIAL IN
0.5321 ---- REACTION
1.5932 ---- 60 FT
4.5578 ---- 330 FT
7.0474 ---- 1/8 ET
098.95 ---- 1/8 MPH

Holly Springs Motorsports

RUN 227   04/30/11 6:31:32 PM
FOOTBRAKE   TT RD #3

LEFT:5867
000.00 ---- DIAL IN
0.5127 ---- REACTION
1.5364 ---- 60 FT
4.4916 ---- 330 FT
6.9908 ---- 1/8 ET
098.34 ---- 1/8 MPH

Holly Springs Motorsports

RUN 234   04/30/11 6:39:23 PM
FOOTBRAKE   TT RD #3

LEFT:5867
000.00 ---- DIAL IN
0.5019 ---- REACTION
1.5288 ---- 60 FT
4.4812 ---- 330 FT
6.9809 ---- 1/8 ET
098.49 ---- 1/8 MPH

Holly Springs Motorsports

RUN 389   04/30/11 8:25:27 PM
FOOTBRAKE   TT RD #6

LEFT:5867
000.00 ---- DIAL IN
0.5281 ---- REACTION
1.5374 ---- 60 FT
4.4821 ---- 330 FT
6.8999 ---- 1/8 ET
099.66 ---- 1/8 MPH

Holly Springs Motorsports

RUN 393   04/30/11 8:29:45 PM
FOOTBRAKE   TT RD #6

LEFT:5867
000.00 ---- DIAL IN
0.5193 ---- REACTION
1.5363 ---- 60 FT
4.4818 ---- 330 FT
6.8992 ---- 1/8 ET
099.69 ---- 1/8 MPH

These ET slips are the result of comparing M/T ET Drag tires (top) to ET Street tires (middle) to ET Street radials (bottom) and displayed in that order with two passes on the same set of tires. The ET Drag tires and ET Street tires are very comparable when you factor in the hour, track temperature, and air temperature. The ET Street Radials with their stiffer sidewall construction and therefore less rolling resistance at the top end made more MPH.

against a pair of ET Street tires (30x12.5x15LT). The ET Street tires weigh 26 pounds while the ET Drag tire weigh 27 pounds. Both tires have a 94-inch circumference and a 10.2-inch tread width.

First, I made two passes using the pair of ET Drag tires (29.5x10.5x15S). It was a typical hot, high-humidity Mississippi day with a late afternoon temperature of 96 degrees F. The two passes were very similar in 60-foot ETs, with 1.6059 and 1.5932 seconds. The eighth-mile ETs were 7.0478 and 7.0474 seconds, respectively, with speeds of 98.94 and 98.95 mph, respectively.

Next, I installed the pair of DOT-approved ET Street tires (30x12.5x15LT) and made two more passes. It was about 1 hour and 10 minutes later and the temperature had cooled to about 88 degrees F, with the direct sunlight off the track, creating a much lower track temperature. Again, the two passes were very similar in 60-foot ETs with 1.5364 and 1.5288 seconds runs, respec-

This is Mickey Thompson's DOT-approved drag radial. These have been the subject of intense research over the past few years, as engineers have been able to find incredible traction while maintaining the relatively stiff sidewall design radials are known for.

tively. The eighth-mile ETs were 6.9908 and 6.9809 seconds, respectively, with the mile per hour being 98.34 and 98.49.

Finally, I installed a set of Mickey Thompson DOT-approved ET Street Radials. A couple of hours had passed, since I had to get the tires mounted and make enough suspension changes to feel I was getting an accurate comparison test. The temperature was now down to 76 degrees F and it was dark. Again, the two passes were very similar in 60-foot ETs with 1.5374 and 1.5363 seconds. The eighth-mile ETs were 6.8999 and 6.8992 seconds, respectively, with the speed being 99.66 and 99.69 mph, respectively. I discussed these runs with several racers I knew were running Mickey Thompson Street Radials, and they all agreed that on a car that dead hooks, they should be worth about a .10 decrease in ET with about one more mile per hour.

Although the weather conditions were minimally different on each pair of runs I feel the ETs show that all three pairs of tires can be quite similar in ETs and speed in a typical full-bodied musclecar like mine with 550 to 600 hp and an automatic transmission. With some further suspension testing, I feel the DOT-approved ET Street Radials could have preformed a little better than shown in the ET slip with more top end speed and therefore a quicker ET. Testing on a lighter weight car instead of my 3,800-pound machine should have also shown a better gain on the DOT-approved Street Radials.

Drag Radial Advice

A car using drag radials in the rear yields a quicker ET than the same car with rear bias-ply slick and

reach up to 2 mph faster quarter-mile times. However, this is only true for cars that dead hook on that radial tire. Radials are far less forgiving than bias-ply slicks. Due to a drag radial's stiffer sidewall construction, they do not recover as easily from a spin as will a bias-ply tire. However, if you take the time to set up your chassis to its full potential and can make the car dead hook with no tire spin, this same stiffer sidewall allows the tire to roll easier. This creates a quicker ET on the far end than its bias-ply counterpart. A car using radial slicks that dead hooks could see up to .100 second reduction in ET with most of the gain on the top end. This is all dependent upon getting that radial tire to hook and stay hooked, as recovery from a spin is unlikely.

Run as much air pressure as possible in a drag radial, which is normally in the 18- to 22-psi range, much higher than its bias-ply slick counterpart at 12 psi. One thing often overlooked when switching from a bias-ply slick to a drag radial is that if both tires have exactly the same rollout (to achieve the same top end speed), the drag radial has to turn more RPM than the bias-ply slick. This is because the bias-ply slick grows (due to the tread pushing outward from centrifugal force) at the far end of the track while the radial does not (due to its stiffer construction).

You may want to pick out a drag radial with a 1- to 1½-inch-larger diameter than the bias-ply slick if you don't wish to turn your engine at a higher engine speed (RPM). Drag race DOT-approved street radials weigh more than a comparably-sized drag slick, but the radial construction has such a low rolling resistance that the

History of Drag Tires

I started drag racing in the mid 1960s, and over the years have had several different drag racing cars. I have seen and used most of the tires available for the sportsman categories. To get the view of someone directly involved with the development side of the first drag tires to the tires we use today, I contacted Gene McMannis. Along with the late Mickey Thompson, Gene has been involved with drag racing tire development since the very beginning. Here is a summary of what Gene had to say:

When Dick Miller asked me to write about drag racing tires, I went through three file drawers of my own records on activities in tire development, and then to the Internet to remember the what, where, and why of things that happened in those early years. Tires were (and are) critical to drag racing. From my search, I found several things were going on simultaneously.

The Beginnings of Competition Racing

Enthusiasts were modifying their cars in the early 1940s. This led to competitions to see whose was the best, sometimes at stop lights, sometimes on neighborhood streets.

Then competitors began blocking off a quiet city street. A starter would drop a flag, and a spotter would identify the winner. In those days, the main street in any town was the "main drag." Street racing became known as "drag racing," a name given by *The Los Angeles Times* newspaper. Under these circumstances, there were many fatalities of both the contestants and observers, so the California Legislature outlawed drag racing.

The Southern California Timing Association (SCTA) ran amateur, timed speed races (usually over a measured mile) on the Muroc and El Mirage dry lakes north of Los Angeles. It added a special quarter-mile track for the first timed drag race using a stopwatch. The first SCTA Speed Week was held at the famed Bonneville Salt Flats in 1949. It was there that racers first began running against the clock (actually a stopwatch) coaxing their vehicles to accelerate faster rather than simply to attain high top speeds.

There were no drag strips (as we know them today) at the time, but there were many emergency landing strips that the federal government had built during World War II. You can't believe how stark they were when first starting out. At these abandoned landing strips, promoters could not set up grandstands or collect fees from the fans. Later on, when the promoters were allowed to set up grandstands, they used the fees to pay prize money to the race winners, eventually growing large enough to foster professional racers with specially-built cars or special dragsters with tubular chassis.

Bob Peterson started *Hot Rod* magazine in 1948 with 5,000 subscribers. It grew fast in those early days. Readers wrote to the editor suggesting a club for drag racing fans. In 1951, the National Hot Rod Association (NHRA) was formed with Wally Parks (the managing editor of *Hot Rod* magazine) as its president and A.K. Miller (president of the SCTA) as its vice president.

The first drag meet, the Santa Ana Drags, began running on an airfield in Southern California in 1950. The NHRA held its first official race in April 1953 on a slice of the Los Angeles County Fairgrounds parking lot in Pomona. In 1955, the NHRA staged its first national event simply called "The Nationals" in Great Bend, Kansas. During the next six years, the Nationals hopped around the country to showcase the growing sport before settling in Indianapolis in 1961.

The Retread Story

Early racing tires were actually retreads of passenger car tires. Today, it is hard to remember that tire retreading was a major industry with a trade group called National Tire Dealers and Retreading Association (NTDRA). Almost all successful tire dealers were also making retreads. The tire carcass (fabric) far outlasted the tread, so it was more economical to replace the tread than to buy a new tire. In the early days of drag racing (pre 1965) the best tires were retreads with a softer compound (rubber). The most popular ones were made by Bruce Tire Company in California. The NTDRA no longer exists. Tire

History of Drag Tires *CONTINUED*

retreading is no longer needed with the longer wearing passenger car tires of today.

Racers reported that the retreaded tires were developing what was known as a "standing wave" at 90 mph. This occurs when the centripetal force exceeds the centrifugal force. We have all seen how a tire grows with speed in a burnout before pulling up to the starting line. This occurs the same way as a car goes down the strip, but it isn't as evident since it happens over a longer period of time. What we don't see is, as the tread goes into contact with the road it is being pushed upward toward the axle. As the speed increases, this force becomes greater.

In the 1940s and 1950s, tire carcasses were made of cotton cord (and later, rayon). These materials had very little elongation (stretch). This standing wave started at 90 mph and got worse as the speed increased. This wave flexes the rubber, which causes heat and destroys the adhesion and carcass, and the tire separates and throws a tread. In the early street drags, it tore up fenders, etc., so the answer was to designate a distance where the top speed would not occur, thus the quarter-mile was selected by early amateur racers.

Sidewall research from 1955 shows a recapped racing slick being tested at 100 mph. The callout for 20 psi shows that engineers were already experimenting with lower pressures for the softer racing tires.

In 1960, Wally Parks went to Akron, Ohio, asking the major tire companies to make "drag tires" for this up-and-coming new sport. At that time, the market was so small, the tire companies could not justify the mold and development costs for such a project.

C. D. Evans was the race consultant to Goodyear. He won his class in the Mexican Road Race in 1954 and was a close friend of the president of the Chevrolet Division of General Motors. M&H was the only maker of drag tires at that time. These were sprint car tires for New England–based racers. Firestone was making its first tire test at its test track in Kingman, Arizona. President Gibson mentioned that Ford was doing the quarter-mile in 14.85 seconds and reaching 102 mph. Ford had produced more than 14,000 specially modified Galaxies for the youth market in the past year. (This was the start of muscle cars out of Detroit.) Prior to that, all modifications were made by individual car owners. Drag racing exploded during this period, partly because of nationwide television coverage.

New Materials

Tire companies had research departments for new rubber polymers and synthetic cord. Racing tires were being made with staple Egyptian cotton, then came Rayon, the strongest cord at the time. This was used on Malcolm Campbell's Blue Bird landspeed record run at Daytona Beach, Florida. The cords loosened during each run, so the tires had to be changed every pass. Adhesion was a problem in these early cords. This changed with the introduction of nylon cord.

Goodyear was the first tire manufacturer to produce a tire with a nylon cord. The earliest race at which it was used was in the 1953–1954 Mexican Road Race (La Carrera Panamerica). This resulted in the first use of nylon on original equipment (OE) production cars, which was on the 1957 Chrysler 300. Nylon became the industry standard in 1958.

The first tires made especially for drag races were recaps. These were slippery in wet weather and were banned by the DOT for highway use. So, everyone had two sets of tires—one for driving to the drag strip and one for competition.

The S/S Innovation

In 1962, Mickey Thompson and I formed a consulting company. In 1963 we incorporated and Max-Trac Development Company later became Max-Trac Tire Company, DBA Mickey Thompson Tires. In 1963, no major tire company was interested in producing drag-specific tires. We were able to convince Cooper Tire to make tires for us as a result of a series of related events.

I had designed the first "Indy Low Profile" tire for Mickey in 1962 for the 1963 Indianapolis 500. It was 24 inches high and 12 inches wide, on a 12-inch-diameter wheel.

Sears was interested in promoting its tires by getting into Indy racing. Mickey and I consulted for them on racing tires. At the time Cooper Tire was trying to get into making tires for Sears. Since Cooper wanted to use our connections at Sears, Cooper agreed to make drag tires

for us. We named them S/S (street and strip) so racers would now need only one set of tires instead of two. Out of this came terms like Street Legal and DOT Approved. These became the first tires in the Sears catalog without the Sears name on them.

The S/S tire became an instant sensation and provided us with sufficient funds for expanding into highway and off-road tires. We started developing dragster tires and were about to go all out when Goodyear decided to make drag tires for top fuel dragsters in 1965. We immediately limited the drag-tire program and stuck with tires for the amateur racer.

And, as they say, the rest is history. I found Gene's information very interesting. I can now better understand how today's tires evolved and why it has been necessary to build the tires of today with their present structure and design.

Here are some Cooper Tire technicians measuring overall tire diameter on some drag slicks in 1965. The 11-inch-wide slicks must have been destined for top fuelers.

History of Drag Tires *CONTINUED*

Area Code 216
928-5986

RETAIL PRICE SHEET
(Federal excise tax effective January 1, 1965)

EFFECTIVE MARCH 1, 1965

MAX-TRAC DEVELOPMENT COMPANY
527 Portage Trail
CUYAHOGA FALLS, OHIO 44221

- "SUPER STOCK" TREAD PATTERN
- PRE-STRESSED CARCASS
- "MAX-TRAC" TREAD
- NYLON PLIES

Super Stock S/S Proven Superior For Street/Strip.

SUPER STOCK *S/S*
WHITE SIDEWALL NYLON TUBE TYPE

TIRE SIZE New	Old	CODE NO.	PRICE	EXCISE TAX
	6.50/7.00-13	341-298-7034	$34.00	$1.96
6.45/6.95-14	6.00/6.50-14	341-298-6544	34.00	1.93
7.35/7.75-14	7.00/7.50-14	341-298-7544	38.50	2.19
8.25/8.55-14	8.00/8.50-14	341-298-8544	42.50	2.12
8.85/9.15-14	9.00/9.50-14	341-298-9544	43.50	2.47
7.35/7.75-15	6.70/7.10-15	341-298-7154	38.50	2.19
8.15/8.45-15	7.60/8.00-15	341-298-7654	42.50	2.26
8.85/9.15-15	8.20/9.00-15	341-298-9054	43.50	2.56

SUPER STOCK *S/S*
BLACK SIDEWALL NYLON TUBE TYPE

TIRE SIZE New	Old	CODE NO.	PRICE	EXCISE TAX
	6.50/7.00-13	311-298-7034	$30.50	$1.96
6.45/6.95-14	6.00/6.50-14	311-298-6544	30.50	1.93
7.35/7.75-14	7.00/7.50-14	311-298-7544	34.50	2.19
8.25/8.55-14	8.00/8.50-14	311-298-8544	38.75	2.12
8.85/9.15-14	9.00/9.50-14	311-298-9544	39.75	2.47
7.35/7.75-15	6.70/7.10-15	311-298-7154	34.50	2.19
8.15/8.45-15	7.60/8.00-15	311-298-7654	38.75	2.26
8.85/9.15-15	8.20/9.00-15	311-298-9054	39.75	2.56

ENGINEERING DATA

TIRE SIZE New	Old	RIM WIDTH	TREAD WIDTH	SECTION WIDTH	OVERALL DIAMETER	SHIPPING WT. White	Black
	6.50/7.00-13	5.0	6.0	7.20	25.1	19.7	19.0
6.45/6.95-14	6.00/6.50-14	5.0	5.5	7.05	25.1	19.7	19.0
7.35/7.75-14	7.00/7.50-14	5.5	6.0	7.85 *7.98*	26.5 *26.6*	20.4 *19.5*	19.5
8.25/8.55-14	8.00/8.50-14	6.0	6.5	8.60	27.7	21.7	20.8
8.85/9.15-14	9.00/9.50-14	6.5	7.0	9.15	28.0	25.2	24.3
7.35/7.75-15	6.70/7.10-15	5.5	6.0	7.85	27.0	22	21.2
8.15/8.45-15	7.60/8.00-15	6.0	6.5	8.25	28.2	23	22.2
8.85/9.15-15	8.20/9.00-15	6.5	7.0	9.15 *9.55*	29.0 *28.86*	26 *26.1*	25

This page from the 1965 Mickey Thompson catalog shows that racing tires more than 9 inches wide were available then. It was the beginning of the outstanding selection of heights and widths we have now.

extra weight is hardly an issue. Tom Kundrik, a Mickey Thompson race technician and drag radial racer himself, says, "Remember, drag radials do not work on all cars. They are very temperamental and require a lot of experimenting and chassis tuning."

Tire Storage

Tires should be stored in a dry place, out of the light (especially florescent and sun light), and away

This is the proper way to stack tires for storage. Notice the much heavier radial tires on the bottom. Thin plywood or very heavy cardboard between the tires spreads weight more evenly, leaving the tires in like-new shape.

from excessive heat and cold. Never leave a tire sitting in water that may freeze. Freezing in water can destroy the tire's tread and compounds. The sun and florescent lights emit ultra-violet (UV) rays which can destroy the tires compound. It is best to keep the tires covered. Do not store tires near welders, furnaces, or high voltage electric motors which give off ozone which again can destroy the tires compound.

If the season is over and your tires are still in good enough shape to start out the new year, remove the tires from the car or jack the car up so the tires are not on the ground. Leaving them in one place for extended periods of time with the car's weight on a particular portion of the tire can destroy the tire's integrity, especially if that tire goes flat and the sidewall is the only thing between the wheel and the surface under the tire. If you run natural rubber tubes as recommended for all non-radial drag tires, this could easily pinch a hole in the tube. Mickey Thompson tires suggest letting the air down to 5 pounds for the storage session.

If the tires are new and not mounted on wheels, store them any way you want following the above guidelines. Don't use them as a shelf to store your transmission on while you have your engine out to freshen up. It's best to keep them in tire racks like at tire stores. But not many of us have that kind of room available or the equipment. They can be stacked on top of each other, as long as they don't squish the lower tires.

I have gotten new tires mail order and they were tied up into much smaller bundles to reduce the box size needed. Boxes so small you would have never guessed there was a big racing tire in them. They never

gave me any trouble. There is a big difference between wading up a new un-mounted tire and wading up a tire at the starting line. If they are stacked up you could put cardboard between them to help distribute the load evenly, but it's not necessary. They can be stacked up or lying down as long as you follow all of the above examples.

Do not use any chemicals on the tires if cleaning is necessary. To clean the sidewalls only use a mild detergent. Never clean the tread surface.

Pressure and Wear

Mickey Thompson Performance Tires suggests the following air pressure as a beginning point for bias-ply drag tires.

Weight (pounds)	Tire Size (diameter in inches)	Pressure (psi)
Under 2,500	Under 32	7 and up
Under 2,500	Over 32	5 and up
2,500 to 3,000	Under 30	10 and up
2,500 to 3,000	30 to 33	8 and up
2,500 to 3,000	Over 33	5.5 and up
Over 3,000	Under 30	12 and up
Over 3,000	30 to 33	8 and up
Over 3,000	Over 33	6 and up

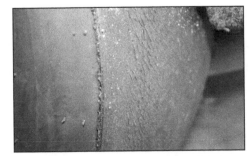

This Mickey Thompson drag slick has been subject to too long of a burnout and overheated, evidenced by the liquid rubber on tire's edge.

This Mickey Thompson drag slick, which has liquid rubber rolled over on edge, shows that the tire needs shorter burnouts, and the feathered edge on tread shows that the tire needs to be rotated side to side more frequently.

This Mickey Thompson ET Street tire needs more air and should have been rotated more frequently side-to-side to get the maximum life from the tire.

Mickey Thompson Performance Tires suggests the following air pressure as a beginning point for Radial drag tires. When working with Drag Radials use 1 psi adjustments. A radial will perform quicker the more air you can run.

Even though this Goodyear slick shows significant tread left, it has been so abused that the tire has gotten very hard and appears to be glazed over.

Weight (pounds)	Tire Size (diameter in inches)	Pressure (psi)
2,500 to 3,000	Under 30	16 and up
2,500 to 3,000	Over 30	8 and up
Over 3,000	Under 30	16 and up
Over 3,000	Over 30	12 and up

Sample Applications

Rear drag tires may need to be screwed to the rim to prevent the wheel from turning inside the tire. This is especially undesirable when running tubes as it pulls the tube's stem through the wheels tube stem hole or rips the stem off the tube or cuts the stem. Either way the tire will go flat and always at the wrong time. The way to be sure if you need to screw the tire to the rim is to use a piece of chalk and draw a line on the wheel and right straight onto the

This Chevelle has too small of a front tire, leaving the front of the car too low and making the front end harder to lift and therefore not getting any weight transfer (pitch rotation).

These rear tires needs more air and the ladder bars are set too aggressively, causing a sidewall tire wrinkle to fold under the tire into the tread (wadding).

This four-link Malibu is wadding the tire tread from too low a rear tire pressure issue and is also hitting the rear tires too hard. This results in not as much tread on the pavement.

This rear tire is wadding up against itself. The car needs better shocks for harder compression and extension.

tire. Watch the marks carefully and inspect after each run. If you see the marks separating between the tire and the wheel screws are needed.

If your car is a dual-purpose car (street/strip) and you don't like the looks of the screws, try screwing the back side only but be sure to do the chalk/shoe polish marking and watching procedure. Otherwise, on a high-horsepower car with sticky tires, save your self a lot of trouble and screw the tires to the rims before you even use them.

For those of you crossing the finish line at an engine speed higher or lower than the desired RPM your engine likes you can change rear end gear ratios or you might consider changing tire diameters.

Although I have stated elsewhere that you should try to run the tallest tire possible for the biggest footprint possible, sometimes it is not needed or the best for your combination.

Let's look at a car running a 26-inch tall tire crossing the finish line in high gear at 120 mph (miles per hour) and a 4.56 rear axle ratio using a transmission with a 1:1 final gear ratio. Let's use the formula:

(Rear Axle Ratio x MPH x Transmisison Output Ratio x 336) / Tire Diameter

We have (4.56 x 120 x 1 x 336) divided by 26, or the engine should be turning 7,071 rpm with a manual transmission or automatic transmission with no converter slippage. Converter slippage can add in the neighborhood of another 300 to 500 rpm or more.

To make this easier let's assume you have a manual transmission. While 7,071 rpm may not be much for a fairly stock small-block short-stroke engine, it could be too much

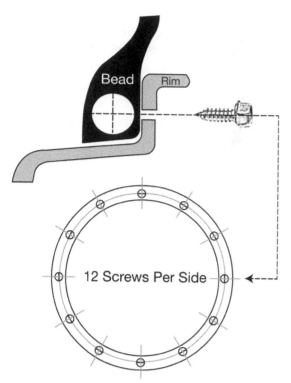

Be sure the screws go into thickest part of tire (avoid going through the tire or into tube) to prevent air leaks.

Racing tires have an extra-thick bead where the tire mounts to the wheel to accommodate screws, which keep the tire from turning on the wheel. Six to eight screws per side of a wheel should be sufficient.

for a fairly stock big-block engine with a much longer stroke. I did an article some time back comparing a small-block Ford rod bearing, main bearing and piston speed (MPH) at 9,000 rpm was about equal to a big block Olds rod bearing, main bearing and piston speed (MPH) at 6,000 rpm because of bearing diameters and a longer stroke.

Let's say we want to reduce our fairly stock big-block engine finish line RPM to about 6,000 rpm without changing gears. Let's use a 30-inch tall tire and the same formula: (4.56 x 120 x 1 x 336) divided by 30, or

the engine should be turning 6,128 rpm with a manual transmission or automatic transmission with no converter slippage. So we now have the desired RPM range without changing the rear gear set and a much bigger footprint on the ground.

Now let's say we have a car running a 30-inch tall tire crossing the finish line in high gear at 120 mph and a 3.73:1 rear axle ratio using a transmission with a 1:1 final gear ratio which would get us to the finish line at 5,013 rpm. But our mildly modified big-block engine had peak horsepower at 6,500 rpm yet we

don't want to go to a smaller tire because the traction is marginal with the 30-inch tall bigger footprint tire on the car now.

Using the same formula with a little trial and error method we can determine the correct gear set without changing the tire diameter. (4.56 x 120 x 1 x 336) divided by 30 or the engine should be turning 6,128 rpm with a manual transmission or automatic transmission with no converter slippage. If we decided to drop the tire diameter instead to 26 inches we would cross the finish line at 7,071 rpm.

FINE-TUNING SUSPENSION FOR MAXIMUM TRACTION

This chapter explains some of the methods to correct or adjust the rear suspension of your ill-handling race car. I discuss methods to improve the car's 60-foot times. Once those are within reason, the rest of the run will be greatly simplified. Don't try to accomplish this by yourself. Speaking from experience you might do a fairly accurate job in a 13-second quarter-mile car, but as your car gets faster it will be much easier and more accurate to track your performance and improvements with another person watching the car.

Shooting Video

The best method short of using a data recorder, (see Chapter 12) is to have the other person record video of the car from a rear corner as it leaves the starting line, focusing in on your hand on the steering wheel. Drivers make instinctive reactions with the steering wheel when the car launches and don't even know it. Having grown up in Michigan and learning how to drive on icy and snowy roads, I have seen many occasions where the race car I was

driving started to turn and I instinctively corrected that turn before I could even think about what was happening. With the front wheels straight, wrap tape of a contrasting color around the steering wheel at the 12 o'clock position so it shows up well in the video. By watching the video of your hand on the steering wheel as the car launches you are able to tell if the car turns left or right (or both) as it leaves the starting line. Many of today's popular NHRA Pro Stock drivers have a white line about 1 inch wide around the top of the steering wheel, so it's obvious they're watching this carefully as well.

If you are turning the steering wheel back and forth, the tires are spinning and the car is not hooking as it should. If the car launches and turns to the right (typical, as discussed in Chapter 1), your car needs more preload. Add small amounts of preload based on how bad the car turned right and test again. Continue adding preload in small amounts and continue testing until the car launches straight and true. If you get to the point where the car

launches and turns to the left, you have too much preload. Remove the preload you last installed and test again.

Having the Right Torque Converter

This discussion assumes your car is in good mechanical tune and you are leaving the starting line at or near maximum torque for your particular engine. Notice I said torque, not horsepower. The torque (not horsepower) makes the car accelerate from a dead stop at a fast rate of speed. Horsepower comes into effect after the car is well on its way and higher in the RPM range.

If you've seen an engine run on a dynamometer, you know that the dyno only measures torque. Horsepower is simply a mathematical function based upon torque and the engine RPM. The dyno is not measuring the horsepower of the engine but simply the torque and RPM and then using a formula to calculate horsepower.

$$HP = (RPM \times Torque) \div 5,252$$

As an example, let's use the engine I have in my car.

Sometimes I have an issue because I have the wrong converter in the car to launch the engine at peak torque value. It was dyno tested and found to have a maximum torque value of 633.9 ft-lbs at 5,000 rpm. Use the formula:

$$HP = (5,000 \times 633.9) \div 5,252$$
$$HP = 603.5$$

As the engine goes faster, torque falls off. But because of the formula, the horsepower continues to rise until the torque really drops off.

At 6,500 rpm, the torque was 540.0. Using the same formula:

$$HP = (6,500 \times 540.0) \div 5,252$$
$$HP = 668.3$$

Any dyno sheet has numbers for each 100 rpm. I have given you the peak numbers, which indicate that

Typical Linear Acceleration Rates

60 feet	330 feet	1/8 mile	1/4 mile	MPH
1.85	7.15	9.00	14.00	92.80
1.82	7.01	8.83	13.75	94.80
1.79	6.87	8.66	13.50	96.70
1.76	6.73	8.49	13.25	98.70
1.73	6.59	8.32	13.00	100.40
1.70	6.45	8.15	12.75	102.30
1.67	6.31	7.98	12.50	104.20
1.64	6.17	7.81	12.25	106.80
1.61	6.03	7.64	12.00	109.50
1.58	5.89	7.47	11.75	112.20
1.55	5.75	7.30	11.50	115.00
1.52	5.62	7.14	11.25	118.00
1.49	5.49	6.98	11.00	121.00
1.46	5.35	6.81	10.75	123.50
1.43	5.22	6.65	10.50	126.00
1.40	5.09	6.49	10.25	130.20
1.37	4.96	6.33	10.00	134.50
1.34	4.83	6.17	9.75	138.10
1.31	4.70	6.01	9.50	141.60
1.28	4.57	5.85	9.25	146.80
1.25	4.44	5.69	9.00	151.20
1.22	4.31	5.53	8.75	156.00
1.19	4.18	5.37	8.50	160.80
1.16	4.05	5.21	8.25	165.60
1.13	3.92	5.05	8.00	170.40
1.10	3.80	4.90	7.75	176.40
1.07	3.67	4.74	7.50	182.40
1.04	3.55	4.59	7.25	188.70
1.01	3.42	4.43	7.00	195.10
0.98	3.29	4.27	6.75	203.70
0.95	3.17	4.12	6.50	212.30
0.92	3.04	3.96	6.25	220.90
0.89	2.92	3.81	6.00	230.00
0.86	2.80	3.66	5.75	243.70
0.83	2.66	3.49	5.50	257.40

You can use this chart to compare your MPH and ET to find your strong and weak parts on a typical acceleration curve.

Driving for many years on slick winter roads can develop great reflexes. They may develop to a point where you don't realize you're making corrections to a race car's unwanted movements at the starting line.

Here's a disassembled view of a competition torque converter. There's a lot of engineering and technology hiding inside them, and the latest offerings from specialists are better than ever. It's now possible to get a converter custom-crafted to meet your exact needs.

this engine needs a torque converter that stalls at 5,000 rpm, and the shift point should be at 6,500 rpm for the fastest possible run.

Since a dyno measures torque and engine speed you know at what RPM the peak torque is for your engine. Your torque converter should stall at or near the peak torque RPM.

According to the TCI Web site: "Converter stall is the RPM that a given torque converter (impeller) has to spin in order for it to overcome a given amount of load and begin moving the turbine. When referring to 'How much stall will I get from this torque converter?,' it means 'How fast (RPM) must the torque converter spin to generate enough fluid force on the turbine to overcome the resting inertia of the vehicle at wide open throttle?' Load originates from two places:

"(1) From the torque imparted on the torque converter by the engine via the crankshaft. (This load varies over RPM, i.e., torque curve, and is directly affected by atmosphere, fuel, and engine conditions.)

(2) From inertia, the resistance of the vehicle to acceleration, which places a load on the torque converter through the drivetrain. This can be thought of as how difficult the drivetrain is to rotate with the vehicle at rest, and is affected by car weight, amount of gear reduction, tire size, ability of tire to stay adhered to ground, and the stiffness of the chassis. (Does the car move as one entity or does it flex so much that not all the weight is transferred during initial motion?)

The primary thing we want to remember about torque converter stall speed is that a particular torque converter does not have a 'preset from the factory' stall speed, but rather its unique design produces a certain range of stall speeds depending on the amount of load the torque converter is exposed to."

My car's torque converter is stalling at 3,850 according to my Sportsman Data Recorder from Racepak. At 3,900 rpm, the torque was 509.5 ft-lbs. The point is that the torque converter needs to match the peak torque RPM

of the engine for the car to launch as hard and as fast as possible. In this case, the car is launching at 1,100 rpm below its peak torque at a loss of 124.40 ft-lbs, resulting in 60-foot clockings about .05 second short of where they should be. The car is still consistent; however, it could be faster. That .05 second removed from the 60-foot clockings could result in a .10 to .15 second quicker ET, and could be a bigger thrill in the ride and probably bring the front wheels up 6 to 12 inches farther.

However, as mentioned previously, if a car is standing on its back bumper it may be getting maximum traction off the line, but not necessarily getting maximum forward acceleration motion. Since the car is pivoting on the rear tires, the front of the car is actually going rearward in order to get to that height and making the car much harder to push forward because of the rearward momentum.

Adjusting Pinion Angle

Pinion angle is measured in reference to the angle of the pinion gear compared to the driveshaft. As I said, to the *driveshaft*, not the ground, transmission, engine, or any of the many other methods I have heard of. While these measurements are important for other reasons, they have nothing to do with pinion angle.

A pinion angle topic discussion has many opinions. Some agree that pinion angle helps a car's launch, while others say it has no effect. To those who feel it has no effect, I always propose the question, "Then why does a car hook harder and have a quicker 60-foot time with more pinion angle?" No one has ever been able to dispute this.

Matching the torque converter to the engine's peak torque RPM results in a harder launch. It's critical to know at what RPM the torque peak occurs, how many ft-lbs of torque are being generated, and how much your car weighs. All of these factors are critical when choosing the best-possible converter.

Before you just go out and throw additional pinion angle into your car, remember that pinion angle robs horsepower as the engine overcomes the angle. The rotation of the driveshaft and pinion gear straightens out the angle and forces it to 0 degrees or flat. This happens no matter how much pinion angle is installed on the car. The more pinion angle there is, the more horsepower needed (or robbed) from the engine (which could be used to accelerate faster).

The effect of this straightening process (moving the pinion angle to zero) creates a leverage affect at the front of the driveshaft and also at the rear end. Using the weight of the car, this drives the tires harder into the pavement.

Cars using no-hop bars or lift bars must have the pinion angle reset

to compensate for the change from installing one of these kits. It is very important to get yourself an angle measuring tool, then check and correct your car's pinion angle.

If you have a factory four-link suspension system, pinion angle can be changed with adjustable upper control arms. By making both arms longer in unison the car loses pinion angle. By making both arms shorter (in unison) the car gains pinion angle. If you have a factory three-link system (torque tube) then the torque tube must have an adjuster to make the changes. With the adjuster at the bottom, you need to lengthen it for more pinion angle or shorten it for less pinion angle. If the adjuster is at the top, you need to do the opposite.

Now you can see why all of my adjusters are double adjustable, meaning no bolts need to be

removed to make adjustments. Just loosen the jamnuts to make adjustments as the adjuster has left-hand threads on one end and right-hand threads on the other end. Be sure to look at the threads when loosening the jamnuts to be sure you are not accidentally tightening them. Single-adjustable adjusters require one end to be removed from the car to make adjustments making the process more difficult and more lengthy.

With factory leaf-sprung cars, wedges can be installed between the axle housing tubes (where the leaf spring mounts) and the leaf springs themselves, thus tipping the pinion either upward or downward depending upon the shim being used and its direction.

Ladder-bar-equipped cars need double adjusters at the rear of the bar, just like a torque tube. With the adjuster at the bottom, you must lengthen both ladder bar adjusters in unison for more pinion angle, or shorten both ladder bar adjusters in unison for less pinion angle. If the adjuster is at the top then you need to do the opposite.

Advanced Chassis puts the adjuster at the top to create less stress, causing the suspension to pull on the adjuster rather than push. Never use bolt-on ladder bars added to the stock

This photo shows the adjustable upper control arm (for setting pinion angle and preload) connected to a plate steel no-hop bar with a track locator. All these components work together to transfer energy to the rear tires. No energy is wasted bending or flexing these components, and their adjustability means you can account for different track and weather conditions, different tires, and even different engine power levels (such as when using nitrous oxide) with just a few under-car adjustments.

These wedges are typical examples of what's used to change pinion angle under vehicles equipped with rear leaf springs. Moving the wedge alters the angle and allows it to be set at the optimal point.

suspension, as this creates a binding situation due to the two different suspension systems having two different arc travel patterns. Bolt-on ladder bars added to the stock suspension definitely get rid of wheel hop, but does so by binding up the rear suspension. They do not allow the suspension to move freely, and this is not ideal for the best-possible traction.

If you have a factory four-link suspension system, pinion angle can be changed with adjustable upper control arms. If preload is adjusted into the car suspension, then the preload must be removed before setting the pinion angle. Notice how many flats must be lengthened in the upper control arm to get it to neutral, then after setting the pinion angle, the passenger side upper control arm can simply be shortened the same number of flats, and the car will have the same preload it had before adjusting the pinion angle. Neutral can be felt as you

are turning the adjuster to get rid of the preload. There will be a spot that the adjuster can be moved back and forth a small amount with your hand using no wrenches.

The bolt should be able to be pushed in and out freely. Also, if you have an anti-roll bar, one or both ends of the anti-roll bar must be unhooked to remove any preload from the anti-roll bar. Remember, all adjustments must be made with the car race ready, setting level on all four tires, and with the driver in the driver's seat or something of equal weight. By making both arms longer in unison the car loses pinion angle. By making both arms shorter (in unison) the car gains pinion angle. Once the pinion angle has been set, the preload can now be set, and then reattach the anti-roll bar in a neutral position.

Cars with lower-horsepower engines and even some cars with higher-horsepower engines may hook satisfactorily and consistently

as they are. For the car that is not giving you the desired 60-foot times or not high enough wheel stands or not consistent enough 60-foot clockings, you should look at your cars pinion angle. With the right settings, pinion angle can make the car hook harder by planting the rear tires with greater force.

Factory pinion angle which is near 0 for longer U-joint life (100,000 to 200,000 miles) needs to be modified. To make pinion angle adjustments, the car needs to be race ready and sitting on all four tires with the driver or someone of similar weight sitting in the driver's seat. Race ready means all tires are the correct pressure, the driver in the driver's seat, all liquids at the proper level, the gas tank at the proper level, etc.

Using an angle finder, measure the driveshaft angle and then the pinion angle. Once you have the driveshaft angle you may need to unbolt the driveshaft to get the pinion angle using the differential yoke that the driveshaft bolts to. Otherwise quite often on the GM rear ends there is a flat spot on each side of the rear cover where the axle tubes are pressed in. This should be machined 90 degrees to the pinion. The driveshaft and the pinion angles together normally make the shape of a very flat letter "V." If so, add the two angles together to get the present pinion angle. Pinion angle is only the difference between the pinion and driveshaft.

From the factory, your car probably has next to 0 degrees of pinion angle. Each car needs its own setting. Too little pinion angle and the car won't hook well. To much pinion angle and the car will hook, but at a loss of horsepower. I suggest a starting point of 2 degrees negative pinion

No-hop bars of the past are too tall and relocate the imaginary intersection point of the upper and lower control arms too far rearward. The DMR no-hop bars are shorter and work well up to about 800 to 1,000 hp.

angle for cars in the 400 hp range and maybe 4 degrees for cars in the 600-hp range and up to 7 degrees for cars running a large shot of nitrous maybe in the range of 1,000 hp or more of combined engine horsepower and nitrous horsepower off the line. Very seldom does any car need more than 7 degrees of negative pinion angle.

When you measure driveshaft angle and pinion angle, adding the two together represents total negative pinion angle.

If you are into time savings and convenience a digital angle finder from Allstar Performance is well worth the extra dollars. Not only is it digital making it much easier to read (1/2-inch-tall LED numbers with two decimal places compared to 1 degree increments on a dial angle finder) it will also rotate the display if the angle finder is needed in an upside-down position so you can easily read the display. It also has a button to turn on a screen backlight and arrows on each end of the display to tell you which end is up and which end is down.

Pinion angle adjustments affect other aspects of the car. Now with a greater bite in the rear, the front of the car should lift higher. If your car squats in the rear, it should squat harder. If it lifts in the rear if may lift even harder. Therefore, any shock adjustments you had previously made may also need to be changed. The point is to get the car's chassis to hit the rear tire as hard as possible and then control that hit to your desired needs with shock settings. That is why I strongly suggest quality double-adjustable shocks front and rear to provide you the ability to set your car's chassis to where it needs to be for your particular combination.

Set the front shocks in about the middle to a loose setting for extension. While testing, keep loosening the extension setting until you reach the desired front-end lift. Remember, you can get a car to lift too far in the front by creating a rearward motion. This rearward motion is similar to the front of the car trying to back up, thus making it harder to move the entire car forward. The compression side adjustment must be stiffer so the car doesn't come down so hard it bounces, thus loading and unloading the rear tires repeatedly.

The rear shocks need to be set differently depending upon whether the car lifts or squats in the rear upon acceleration. For a starting point, a car that squats in the rear should have the rear shocks set fairly loose on compression to allow as much squat as possible, yet fairly stiff upon extension to help control wheel hop. A car that lifts in the rear will be opposite, but remember that even though the car is trying to lift in the rear you also want to get weight transfer (pitch rotation) and too stiff of a compression setting will not allow this to happen.

Also take into consideration that when setting the car's rear shocks, a car that lifts in the rear (since the rear of the car is lighter than the front of the car) can lift before the front, thus making it impossible for the front to lift, resulting in no weight transfer (pitch rotation). With quality adjustable shocks you can control this and make it work to the car's advantage.

Adjusting Chassis Preload with Rear Coil Springs

In cars with rear coil springs using a factory four-link setup (two

upper control arms and two lower control arms), preload can be accomplished in many different ways. One way is to install air bags inside the coil springs. A typical starting point for air pressure is 25 psi in the passenger side with 5 psi in the driver's side. If the car moves to the right upon launch, more air is needed in the passenger-side bag. If the car moves left upon launch, less air is needed in the passenger-side bag.

Custom rear coil springs are offered by many manufacturers, offering a stronger spring in the passenger side than the driver's side. There is not much you can do if the springs are not right for your car's application except find a spring the same size with a stronger or weaker pounds-per-inch rating for the passenger side of your car. These advertisements lead you to believe that any 1970 Chevelle with a big-block engine needs the same spring as another, regardless of torque and horsepower.

That is simply not true. A combination of both custom springs and air bags may be used. The disadvantage to either of these methods is that by preloading the passenger-side rear corner with an air bag, a taller spring, or both, you are also raising that same corner and pushing down on the opposite (driver's side) front corner. This hinders the maximum weight transfer possible, but should correct crooked launches.

A better way to set preload in cars with rear coil-springs using a factory four-link setup (two upper control arms and two lower control arms) is once the pinion angle has been set adjust the passenger-side upper arm shorter than the driver-side control arm. This preloads the chassis getting rid of the typical GM right turn off the starting line.

This method allows you to install preload into the chassis, and also gives you adjustability of preload without greatly sacrificing ride or chassis movement as air bags or trick springs will. This method allows for no air bags and the same spring to be used on both rear corners and does not eat up suspension travel as preloading with a heavier spring on the passenger side or heavier air pressure in an air bag. Shorten the passenger side upper control arm one to two complete turns for preload. Start with one turn (also referred to as six flats because of the six-sided adjuster).

If the car now turns right upon launch shorten the passenger-side upper control arm more. If the car now turns left upon launch lengthen the passenger-side upper control arm. Work up on it slowly until the car launches in a straight line. Don't run any more preload than necessary or the car will not drive in a straight line. Now you can see why all of my adjusters are double adjustable, meaning no bolts need to be removed to make adjustments. Just loosen the jamnuts to make adjustments as the adjuster has left-hand threads on one end and right-hand threads on the other end. Be sure to look at the threads when loosening the jamnuts to be sure you are not accidentally tightening them. Single adjustable adjusters require one end of the control arm to be removed to make adjustments making the process more difficult and more lengthy.

Don't forget that just as 1,000 hp is an arbitrary point at which a car needs the imaginary intersection point out much further in front of the neutral line it can also be used as an arbitrary point that a car can turn left at the starting launch instead of right. The need for preload is based upon power with the more powerful cars needing the passenger side arm longer and the less powerful cars needing the passenger side shorter. It seems like cars in the low-9- to high-8-second range can be run without preload. Slower than that, they need the upper passenger side arm shorter. Faster than that, they need the upper passenger-side arm longer. Adjusting the passenger-side control arm longer is the same as adjusting the driver-side arm shorter. Adjusting the passenger-side control arm shorter is the same as adjusting the driver-side arm longer.

Adjusting one of the upper control arms, shorter to create preload, cocks the rear end a little out of square under the car. Depending upon how tight the fit is for the rear tires in the wheel well openings this can cause an interference between the tires and frame or body. Just as pinion angle goes away under acceleration so will the preload set using this method. Even with the rear end being square under the car bias-ply drag tires will grow (get narrower and taller) at the far end of the track. Be sure this is not an issue for your car.

Bias-ply tires also get shorter and wider as they become more used thus not only changing effective gear ratio but also again changing tire clearance. Sometimes sacrifices must be made. I have my car setup with the biggest tire physically possible to get under the car. When new the tires fit fine. As they become more used they start to rub a little on the 3-inch tailpipes while turning corners. Rather than run a smaller tire I choose to let them rub. When I get new tires I just repaint the tail pipes and start over.

While not necessarily recommended, and depending upon how bad they rub, the same can be done if your car's tires rub from setting

Even if your tires clear everything while sitting still, the car's body will roll going around corners and create an issue. This tire is hitting the tail pipes but it is minimal, and if a different offset wheel would not work I would let it happen as opposed to using a narrower tire.

preload. However, depending upon how your upper control arms are made you could use some hardened shims and try to relocate the rear end to one side. If both sides are rubbing you may have to go to a narrower tire but the sacrifice will be well worth it for a good straight line launch. Another way to correct it without going to smaller tires would be to install an anti-roll bar. Remove enough preload to allow the tires to clear and then add additional preload with the anti-roll bar.

Many of the late 1960s and early 1970s GM performance cars came from the factory already having the passenger side rear corner higher than the driver-side rear corner. You could switch springs side-to-side and still have the same stance. Springs should be installed and used for a few days to settle in before determining if you need to make any adjustments. If you have this problem, or are using either air bags, trick springs, or both, this stance can be mostly eliminated

by cutting 1/3 to 3/4 of a turn off the passenger front coil spring.

Never use heat to lower a spring, as it ruins the spring by changing the temperament of the metal. Instead, use a high-speed cut-off wheel. This is a lot of work, since you need to carefully remove the coil spring each time you cut it, but it's worth the effort once you're done. Take small amounts at a time. If you cut too much off at once, you'll be buying a new spring. This can be a very dangerous job and should not be attempted unless you have experience and the right tools.

Cars with rear suspension setups that lift in the rear (like no-hop bars or lift bars) should never use the air bag or trick-spring method. Doing so uses up most of the upward suspension travel in the rear suspension, leaving none left for the launching of the car. Also, never use air shocks in a drag car unless you have a 600-pound tool box you plan to leave in the car while racing (not allowed or recommended).

Adjusting Chassis Preload with Rear Leaf Springs

For cars with leaf springs, there is more than one way to accomplish preload. Traction bars (sometimes called slapper bars) are the most common method used. A slapper bar gets its name because it bolts to the existing spring U-bolts, replacing the plate under the spring and extending forward. There are many different versions of these traction bars for leaf springs. A gap is left between the snubber on the end before it hits the spring. The gap can be different on both sides before slapping the frame, thus creating preload.

Also available for most brand leaf spring cars are Chrysler Super Stock springs. The name came from the fact they were developed in the late 1960s by Chrysler for NHRA Super Stock race cars. They have a heavier spring rate on the passenger's side than the driver's side, thus creating preload. Additionally, they are much stiffer in the front half of the spring than the rear half, creating a rear suspension that works like a ladder-bar setup. I have used these style springs in a GM

This ultra-tall front coil spring has been cut (shortened) by one full coil to adjust the vehicle's ride height. Getting the proper level stance is important to both weight transfer and aerodynamics.

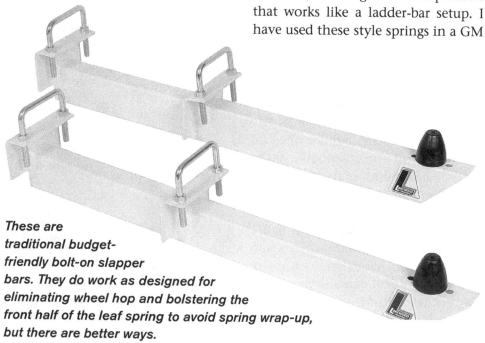

These are traditional budget-friendly bolt-on slapper bars. They do work as designed for eliminating wheel hop and bolstering the front half of the leaf spring to avoid spring wrap-up, but there are better ways.

Oldsmobile Omega race car and they worked great. See more about these springs in Chapter 2.

Adjusting Rear Rise or Squat

A car that lifts in the rear upon acceleration plants the tire harder than a car that squats in the rear. As I stated earlier, you can't pick up 100 pounds without putting 100 pounds of extra pressure on your feet. A car transferring weight from front to rear (pitch rotation) and then lifting in the back puts extra pressure on the rear tires when compared with a car that squats in the rear.

For cars with rear coil springs using a factory four-link setup (two upper control arms and two lower control arms), the imaginary intersection point of the upper and lower control arms (if extended forward) can be adjusted to make the car lift or squat in the rear. If the imaginary intersection point of the upper and lower control arms is above the neutral line, the rear of the car pushes up on the body upon launch, therefore pushing down harder on the tires, planting the rear tires more effectively and eliminating wheel hop. The closer this imaginary intersection point is to the rear-end housing the harder the chassis hits the rear tire.

Keep in mind that you can hit a tire too hard. If the imaginary intersection point of the upper and lower control arms is below the neutral line, the car squats in the rear and therefore is not pushing down on the tires as effectively.

For cars with rear coil springs using a factory four-link setup (two upper control arms and two lower control arms), the imaginary intersection point of the upper and lower control arms can be changed by alter-ing the angle of the upper or lower control arms. Cast-iron no-hop bars have been around for years that raise the back of the upper control arms and greatly shorten the imaginary intersection point of the upper and lower control arms bringing it on the top side of the neutral line.

Thirty years ago full-bodied cars with much less tire bite and lower horsepower levels responded well to these changes. By causing the car to lift in the rear you not only planted the tire harder but you eliminated wheel hop. The original-design no-hop bars are too tall with today's horsepower levels and cause the suspension to hit the tire too hard. I have spent more than 30 years perfecting no-hop bars and have achieved the right height with my shorter plate steel no-hop bar that work with today's much higher-horsepower cars. Being shorter, the upper control arm is not changed so radically and does not hit the tire as hard.

You can overpower a tire and set it into spin mode if you hit it harder than the tire is engineered to take. Any time you switch to no-hop bars of any style you must add adjustable upper control arms to reset the pinion angle or it will be farther from where it should be than it already was with factory control arms.

For a short time there was a company that made lift-bars. These lowered the rear of the lower control arm. This method moved the intersection point above the neutral line using the same principle as the no-hop bars, but they did not intersect at the optimum location. They worked well on some cars and at some tracks, but not all the time at every track. Because of the different imaginary intersection point created, these bars were too drastic and also hit the tire too hard, just like the taller cast-iron no-hop bars. Today, they are no longer being made nor is the company still in business. I tried them when installing non-GM rear ends in GM cars. Now you can get a weld-on no-hop bar when installing non-GM rear ends in GM cars, leaving the lower control arms in the factory location.

Several aftermarket rear-axle suppliers have raised the upper mount location; however, it is raised less than 1 inch. This is not enough to make a significant difference, and a no-hop bar is still needed. If possible, have the upper mount attached at the factory height (based upon the

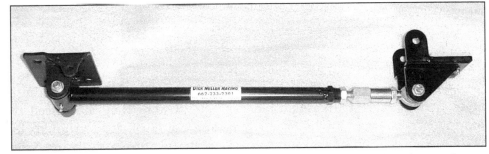

This leaf-link traction bar accomplishes the same function as the slapper bar, but does so with better quality components and the added adjustability provided by the turn barrel at the front of the arm. Note the greasable polyurethane bushing at the rear of the arm. This arm is for GM S-series pickup trucks, and has proven to be effective over the years. Once the S-series trucks are treated to increased power, some form of traction control becomes essential.

axle tube centerline) and add weld-on no-hop bars.

For cars with rear coil springs using a factory three-link setup (a torque tube and two lower control arms), the shorter wheelbase changed the imaginary intersection point of the torque tube and lower control arms to a point that the car already rises in the rear and works great as is.

Front mounts for ladder-bar suspensions normally have multiple vertical adjustment holes. Squat or rise can be adjusted using the neutral line drawing, which is used for a reference point when considering rear rise or squat in suspended cars. The front mount for the ladder-bar car is the reference point to be used when making the necessary adjustments to achieve rise or squat.

Rear leaf-spring-equipped cars need to follow the same procedure as ladder-bar cars when making adjustments for rise or squat. They may be adjusted by either changing the front spring mount or rear spring shackle/mount. This is discussed further in Chapter 2.

Adjusting Anti-Roll Bars

Notice this section is titled adjusting anti-roll bars, not sway bars. There is a difference.

Sway bars (both front and rear) should be removed completely from pure drag racing cars. Sway bars (either front or rear) help with body roll under hard cornering. On a mild-horsepower car (300 hp or less) with a relatively unmodified system, a sway bar may help since its basic purpose is to mask the fact that there is a problem on one corner of the car. It does this by transferring 50 percent of the problem to the other side. It's a bandage, not a fix.

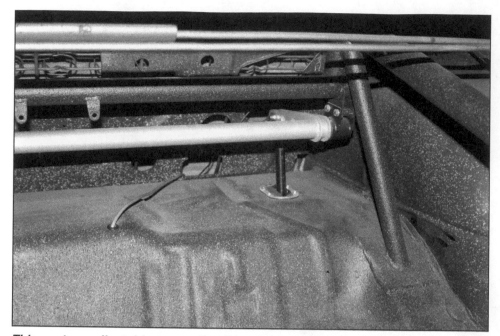

This custom adjustable rear anti-roll bar is mounted in the trunk of a GM A-Body. These bars allow you to set the amount of tension you want, helping equalize each side of the rear suspension. Most high-powered (600-plus hp) cars can benefit from the use of these anti-roll bars.

Anti-roll bar kits are installed on the rear of the car and are welded to the frame, with upright arms connecting to the rear housing. Reacting similar to torsion bars (see Chapter 8), anti-roll bars use a twisting motion to apply pressure through the frame to keep the front of the car level for more even weight transfer to the rear tires. Additionally, it helps stop the body from twisting permanently under severe conditions. More weight transferring evenly to the rear tires provides better straightline traction by giving equal bite to both rear tires. Because of the twisting they are forced to endure, anti-roll bars should be made from chrome-moly material due to its ability to twist and untwist better than mild steel.

Anti-roll bars can be installed in front of or behind the rear axle, but the upright bars must be as close to the outside (left and right) of the rear-end housing as possible. For those who don't have enough room under the car to install an anti-roll bar, trunk-mounted anti-roll bars are available that have the uprights going down through the coil springs. This leaves room underneath the car for a large-diameter exhaust system and a factory gas tank. If you do not have a chassis roll bar mounted in the car, other versions are available with a tripod setup that bolts everything into the trunk.

Anti-roll bars should be adjusted only after all other suspension setups are complete. The driver (or equal weight) must be in the driver's seat. The car must be resting on all four tires, inflated to race pressure. There should be no preload set into the anti-roll bar. It should be installed with no preload. Lengthen or shorten the upright bars until the bolts slip fit through the heim joints and through the tabs welded to the rear-end housing. If any suspension changes are made (including preload), the anti-roll bar must be checked again for a neutral setting.

Adjusting Front and Rear Tire Pressure and Diameter

Front tire pressure as well as tire height can affect reaction times. If your reaction times are not what they should be, you can try different tire pressures and/or different tire diameters. These influence the rollout of the car before a red light occurs.

Rear tire pressure is different for each car combination and may require adjustment based on the track conditions and temperature. Normally, a good starting point for bias-ply racing tires is in the range of 11 to 13 pounds, while drag radial tires prefer the added pressure of 18 to 22 pounds, which also helps create a stiffer sidewall. These pressures are starting points, since there are many variables.

A low-horsepower car may need more tire pressure to keep the tire from sticking too much and bogging the car down. A high horsepower car may need less pressure to make the tire work and stick harder. A high-horsepower car may like tubes to stiffen the sidewall even more.

Wheel width also affects the optimal tire-pressure point. A wider wheel can cause the tire tread to cup in the center by separating the side walls farther apart, therefore needing more air to flatten out the tire tread again. A narrow wheel can cause the tire tread to bulge outward in the middle from bringing the sidewalls closer together therefore needing less air to flatten the tire tread again.

After racing, check the tread depth to be sure of even wear from side-to-side. If it's not even, there may be a tire pressure issue. Too much wear on the outside edges indicates that the tires need more air pressure. Too much wear in the middle indicates that the tires need less. I am talking small changes here in all of these examples—1 to 2 pounds.

Scaling a Car

Cars are scaled on all four corners to get the best traction possible. Traction is the friction developed between the drive tires and the surface they are trying to grip. The best traction possible needs both drive tires to grip the surface equally.

First make sure that the surface you are using is flat and level (shim the scales to be level if necessary). Next, just as with setting pinion angle and preload, make sure that everything is in the car and where it will be when you go down the track (fuel, water, nitrous oxide, batteries, and driver's weight). Do any kind of alignment on the front or rear before you weigh the car, as well as any ride height adjustments that you want to make. Check all tire pressures and set them to the race settings.

To be sure your scales are level you can use an old trick taught to me many years ago by a contractor while hanging a suspended ceiling.

1. Get a piece of clear plastic tubing about 11 feet long. Fill it (except about 3 inches from each end) with a colored substance (e.g., water with an ample amount of red food coloring). Plug each end to keep the liquid in the tube.

2. Make two wood bases, about 4 x 4 inches. Nail an upright (1 x 1 inch, and 6 inches tall) from the bottom side of the base to the base. Mark the uprights starting at the base in graduated increments (e.g., 1/8 inch) on both uprights making sure the marks on both uprights are measured the same from the base up.

3. Fasten the plastic tube to the uprights, even with the top mark on the upright, being sure both ends of the tube are fastened on the same corresponding mark as the other end.

4. Place one of the base-and-upright combinations on one scale and the other set on another scale. The liquid centers itself just like a bubble in a level. Reading the liquid on each upright tells you if the scales are level or if they need to be moved up or down to be level with the other scale.

Dan Bowers from Advanced Chassis says, "The object of scaling a car is to counteract the natural forces (preload) that work on a car's suspension to make it turn right or left on the starting line. In cars with less than 1,000 hp (an approximate arbitrary number or point at which the car's chassis reactions change), you are adding weight to the right rear tire to counteract the driveshaft rotating the rear-end housing. The pinion gear rotation puts a down-force on the ring gear fastened solid on the driver's side of the rear-end housing, and the twisting motion tries to lift the passenger-side wheel while planting the driver-side wheel into the pavement. The result is more traction on the driver's side, making the car want to turn to the right.

"A good starting point for 800-hp cars is around 30 pounds heavier on the passenger tire than on the driver's side. If the car still goes to the right add more preload (weight). If the car goes to the left, take away some preload. A strange thing happens when you approach 1,000 hp and above, the clockwise rotation of the engine toward the passenger side overcomes the forces of the driveshaft turning the corner, and now lifts the driver-side wheel—planting the passenger-side wheel into the ground. This makes the car go to negative, or reverse, preload. This means you actually want to make the passenger-side tire weigh less than the driver-side tire.

"How do you actually make tires heavier? Cars equipped with four link-style rear suspension systems are generally the easiest cars to make preload adjustments to, as these cars are usually based on a full chassis with all of the components easily accessible.

"To add preload, you unhook any anti-roll bar (just one side), or you can 'keep up' with your adjustments by re-centering the link after each adjustment so there is no tension on the anti-roll bar. Just about all of this can be done by simply shortening the top passenger bar on the four-link to add preload or lengthen it to reverse preload.

"The trick is to get your preload without having your car all jacked up on the passenger's side. If you find this condition, you can also add or take away preload by jacking up the left front (driver's side) spring on the car to add weight to the right rear. This accomplishes the same thing without your ride looking funny. You can also lower the right front (passenger's side) spring to accomplish the same thing depending on what the car 'needs' to look right.

"It doesn't really matter how you do this, the car doesn't care how you put the weight there. The only thing that really matters is that you get the weight differential between the two rear tires."

Shims are used under the scale to level the car while it's being weighed. This is critical to getting accurate scale readings. If your scale readings are off because the vehicle isn't level, any changes you make will be less than optimal. Take the time to level out the car to make sure your readings are accurate.

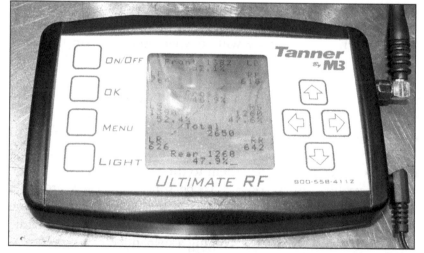

This is a typical scale readout monitor. It shows the actual weights and percentages on each tire, in addition to the cross-corner readings, left- and right-side comparisons, front-to-rear comparisons, and total vehicle weight (2,650 pounds in the center).

For drag racing purposes, the rest of the weights are inconsequential. It is ideal to have more weight on the rear tires and less weight on the front tires. A front-heavy car is hard to keep hooked up. A rear-heavy car can do excessive wheel stands. The more weight there is in a car, the more weight there is to transfer (pitch rotate). Therefore, a heavy car is easier to wheel stand than a lighter car. That's why heavier cars probably like tubes in the slicks as well as they should like drag radials.

This 1987 Olds Firenza boasts a full-tube chassis and is a dedicated track-only car that runs in the popular Super Gas class. It's owned by Paul and Rose Richardson and is very competitive and consistent. Here it's being weighed at all four corners by the specialists at Advanced Chassis before adding upgrades.

To be completely accurate, cars should be rolled onto scales. The rear could be jacked up and the scales slid underneath, but when you jack up the front the front tires arc (with camber), and when placed back down there is a side load on the sidewalls of the tires tipping the scales.

Making the right tuning adjustments can make the difference between a very competitive car and an average car. Just like fine-tuning your engine on the dynamometer can usually result in a easy 20- to 25-hp gain, fine-tuning your chassis on a set of scales allows the car to make use of that extra horsepower. After all, what good is that extra horsepower you just built (or purchased) if the chassis can't use it?

MAKING A PASS

This chapter explains the fundamentals of making a pass down the quarter- or eighth-mile drag strip from the beginning to the end. I then analyze a time slip and explain what it is telling you.

The Burnout

For the bracket racer, burnouts are a method of preparing the tires for maximum traction at the launch.

The first thing you need to accomplish to execute a run is to make a burnout, warming up the rear tires.

To make a good water burnout, the water sprayed on the track (water box) must be evenly distributed so that both tires have an equal amount of water to spin in, and so both tires exit the water at the same time. Optimally, you have a line lock (an electrical switch spliced into the front brake lines that holds brake pressure to the front tires, effectively locking them in place while the rear tires are free to spin).

There are right ways and wrong ways to accomplish a burnout. Here is the right way:

1. Drive your front tires through the water box.
2. When the rear tires first contact the water, rev the engine enough to spin the tires over, being sure the entire rear tire is covered with water.
3. Drive the rear tires into the burnout box until they are at the back edge of the water, closest to the starting line, and stop there.
4. Activate the line lock switch and pump the brakes hard two or three times to build enough pressure so the front brakes do not slip.
5. Shift your transmission into high gear. You can safely do this before the burnout and reduce the engine wear and tear by making the burnout at a much lower engine speed (4,000 to 5,000 rpm).
6. Remove your foot from the brake pedal.
7. At the appropriate time (when the track worker gives you the hand signal), rev up the engine to start the burnout.

To be consistent, burnouts must be identical every time. That means revving the engine to the same RPM for the same length of time on each burnout. It also helps to have a buddy watching you and letting you know when to release the line lock to end the burnout. Depending upon the direction the wind is blowing, it may be difficult for you to tell when the burnout is complete from inside the car. An experienced person outside the car can see the smoke from the tires and can better determine when the burnout is complete.

With the transmission in final gear and the RPM limiter set at 4,000 rpm and hooked to my line lock, floor the engine. Count out about 4 seconds and release the line lock. Before releasing the switch, lift your foot enough that the engine does not rev too high, and lift on the accelerator just as the car starts to move. Do not stop spinning the tires while still in the water or they will cool down again.

Of course, there are variables. The amount of water under the tires greatly affects the burnout. Smoke (steam) appears while spinning the tires. The first smoke is white. As the water disappears, the tires get warmer and the smoke turns to blue. The amount of blue smoke produced is the determining factor as to when the burnout is complete. When both tires are producing steady and equal plumes of blue smoke, the burnout is done. Both tires are clean and equally hot, which is the goal.

That is how to make a good burnout for a Goodyear tire.

However, different manufacturer's tires require different techniques. Mickey Thompson bias-ply tires require a much shorter burnout—about one half as much. A Mickey Thompson radial tire requires even less. Consult with your tire manufacturer as to the burnout needed for the brand and style of tire you are using. Every car's needs are different. Just as different cars need different tire pressures each car also has its own needed length of burnout necessary for best results. Experiment! Most drivers stay in the burnout too long probably because its just too much fun.

Once you have completed your burnout, release the line lock while easing up on the accelerator, but do not completely take your foot off the pedal until the car has moved forward enough to be sure you're not stopping on wet pavement. If you do stop in wet pavement or standing water, the tires instantly cool back down, defeating the purpose of the exercise.

Once you have pulled out of the burnout box and away from the water, never perform a dry hop, or short burnout, on the dry pavement. It may seem like fun or a good way to test your traction, but, you will remove the chemicals that the burnout procedure has brought to the surface of the tire and the car will not hook as good once you reach the starting line. You've got one really great launch ready to go right after the burnout, so don't waste it on a dry hop before the race even begins.

It is possible to overheat the slicks on a burnout. I mentioned that chemicals come to the surface of the tread during the burnout to create a stickier tire. Overheating the tires brings more of those chemicals than necessary to the tire's surface and wastes them on that run. Tires that have been overheated multiple times may no longer work effectively, even though they feel soft and have sufficient tread left. Spin the tires just long enough for them to generate steady, even plumes of smoke, and then move on. This technique helps get the most life and traction from your expensive drag slicks. Remember to rotate your slicks weekly.

Notice the blue smoke starting to roll out under this car during a burnout.

Why Do a Burnout?

Three things need to happen to properly and consistently prepare your tires for the launch:

1. Sticky racing slicks pick up anything loose on the ground they may run over, from leaves or stones to cigarette butts. There is always plenty of loose material on the ground for your slicks to encounter while driving up to the staging lanes. The tires must be cleaned in the water.

2. The burnout heats the rubber to make the compound warmer and softer, which makes it adhere better to the starting line surface.

3. Warming the tires helps bring compounds in the tire to the surface to create a stickier tire.

Street Tires

Not everyone drag races on slicks. For DOT-approved tires, the burnout process is a bit different. While you still want to get them nice and warm, you want to move forward more in the burnout box before beginning the burnout. This is because water can get caught in the treads of the tire, and be held there until after the burnout. When you roll forward to the starting line, the water drains to precisely where you don't want it—underneath your rear tires.

Many savvy racers with treaded tires drive around the burnout box to avoid the water puddles completely, and then back up until the rear tires are on wet pavement. This allows them to accomplish a burnout without picking up water in the tire's treads, and it's a good idea if you're not running slicks.

In addition, not all drag radials require a big smoky burnout to get warm. A smaller burnout works just as well, and five to ten revolutions on the tire is plenty to clean off the debris and get them sufficiently warm. If you're running drag radials or other DOT-approved treaded tires, experiment with shorter burnouts to find the optimum point for traction.

Remember, the shorter your burnouts are, the longer your tires will last. If there's no measurable gain from doing a long, smoky burnout, save your money and just do what's necessary to achieve maximum traction.

Reaction Time

Leaving the starting line on time is critical to successful drag racing. Of course, you want to leave as soon as the light turns green, but no sooner.

I assume that the track where you are racing is using a .500 tree, and with .500 being a perfect reaction time. A .500 tree has three yellow lights and a green light, all spaced exactly .500 second apart. Red lights (leaving before the green or go light) are .499 or less. In foot-brake racing, a reaction time in the mid .520s wins most races if the car runs on its dial-in. However, a quicker reaction time should give you a little advantage at the finish line in case your car slows down or picks up on that run.

In the classes where transmission brakes are allowed, a mid-to-high .500s light is very common (and even necessary) to go through many rounds. If you are running a class with a .400 "Pro" tree, there is only one yellow light, followed by a green light .400 second later. Everything else is identical, except a perfect light is based on .400 second not .500 second.

Cutting consistently good reaction times takes a lot of practice and a lot of testing to see what works best. Of course, your car must be consistent. If your car's ETs are all over the place there is no way your reaction times at the starting line will be consistent. If you asked another racer what you need to do at the starting line, he would probably tell you, "Pull up to the starting line until you turn on both yellow lights and then leave on the last yellow. If you wait until the green light comes on, you will be too late and lose the race." While this is true, there are many variables, including staging and track position, that can be adjusted to make your reaction time more consistent.

Staging

You may shallow-stage your car, deep-stage your car, or anything in between.

At the starting line, there are two or three photocells mounted in the outside retaining walls at ground level. Each has an accompanying reflector in the middle of the track.

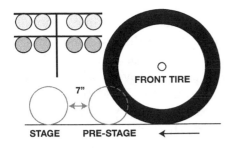 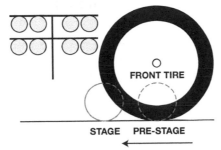 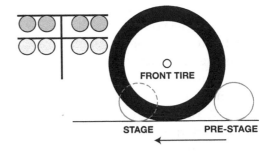

This front tire has just broken the pre-staged beam. Wait for your opponent before going any farther.

This front tire has now broken the staged beam and is ready to race. The amount you roll through and still have both beams broken helps determine the 60-foot clockings and the reaction time.

This front tire has broken the staged beam and no longer is breaking the pre-staged beam representing a deep stage. You must write "deep stage" on your window by your dial-in for the control tower to see.

Your front tire must break the beam from the photocell going across the track to the reflector in order to turn on the appropriate light on the tree.

Here is a good procedure to follow:

1. Slowly approach the "pre-stage" (first) beam, riding the brake pedal until you just get the light to illuminate. If you approach the pre-stage beam too quickly, you have no control over where the front tire stops or any idea how much farther it is to the next beam. Most tracks have (and enforce) a "no back up" rule, so if you travel too far past the lights you are not allowed to back up. Even if you could, your opponent is already staged and you would not have enough time before the tree goes to green.

2. Come to a complete stop before moving toward the staged (second) beam. Courtesy says you should be sure your opponent has also turned on his or her pre-stage beam before you continue to the staged beam.

You have exactly 7 inches between the pre-stage beam and the staged beam. If you allow your car to roll forward exactly 7 inches,

breaking the staged beam, the next pair of yellow stage lights on your side of the tree light up and you are now staged. If you stay in that location on the track it is referred to as being "shallow staged." Most drivers stay there so they can consistently be in the same location on the track for each run. If you have a slow-leaving car, you may want to let it move slowly forward until the pre-stage beam is out.

3. If the pre-stage light goes out, your car is now "deep staged." This also allows the car to be consistently in the same location on the track for each run.

You must have the word "DEEP" written on the glass of your car along with your car number and dial-in-time to deep stage. This tells the person activating the tree that after you have turned on the pre-stage and stage beams, to allow you some time to roll even farther forward until your top pre-stage beam goes out.

It is also important to deep stage slowly so you don't allow the car to roll too far forward and let the stage beam photocell make contact with its reflector, which gives you a red light.

4. Some tracks have a third photocell and reflector set called the "guard" beam. If you break this beam before the green light, you get a red light.

This beam is exactly 13 inches from the staged beam. It is used to ensure competitors don't roll forward an unfair amount, which shortens the measured start-to-finish distance and allows an advantage. This guard beam also prevents you from running front tires so tall that they also shorten the measured start-to-finish distance, allowing you to get to the finish line quicker than you should.

Ideally, if you leave when the final yellow light comes on, you should have a .500-second reaction time. Staging shallow or deep as described above may not even get you close to a .500-second light. Every driver and car has different response times, which are combined for the overall reaction time.

Track Position

You need to find the best-possible spot on the track to start the run. When experimenting, you must repeat the run at least two times to be sure you can repeat the data. I continue to assume your car is consistent (see Chapter 12). Staging shallow or deep is the only method that is consistent, but you may stage your car somewhere in between if you are confident you can get back to this exact position repeatedly and you have no more mental, physical, or mechanical adjustments to be made.

Make two runs staged shallow at exactly the same spot while reacting to the tree at exactly the same time. Then, also reacting to the tree exactly the same, make two runs staged deep at exactly the same spot.

The pair of runs should be identical. If not, make three to five runs each instead of two each. Average the first shallow runs, and then average the second deep runs. The difference between the averages is how much your reaction time can be affected by staging "somewhere in between" shallow staging and deep staging.

Once you find your spot, practice until you can get the car in exactly the same spot every time.

Mechanical Snafus

Most mechanical items that can negatively impact reaction times can be improved upon by repeated testing and subsequently finding the best settings for your car.

Tire Sidewall Stiffness

When a tire hooks, it takes time for the sidewall to wrap up (wrinkle) before the car starts moving forward. The heavier the car and the more power it has, the more wrap there is in the tire. Manufacturers make tires with different sidewall stiffnesses. More air pressure also stiffens the sidewall but be careful not to over-inflate the tire and cause the tire to crown. This causes the tire to not have as much tire contact surface touching the ground.

Carburetor

Based on the chassis and carburetor being used, adjustments may help with reaction times. The carburetor linkage may be adjusted at the accel-erator or at the carburetor to increase or decrease reaction time. The point where the accelerator cable attaches to the carburetor throttle shaft linkage can be moved, affecting reaction time. Mounting the accelerator cable closer to the pivot center of the throttle shaft yields quicker response times. Likewise, the farther away the accelerator cable is mounted to the pivot center of the throttle shaft, the slower the response time. Similar adjustments may also be made at the accelerator.

Carburetor tuning also affects the launch, so you need to find out the answers to these questions: Are the secondaries coming in too slow? Is the mixture too lean with no power or rich and not clean? Is it the right size (cfm) carburetor? and make the appropriate adjustments.

Suspension Setup

The front and rear suspension setup can greatly affect reaction times.

Is the car moving forward upon launch, or wasting time with a huge

Mental Stress

Mental stresses can undoubtedly affect reaction times. They can be relieved once you recognize which ones are affecting you. For instance, did you have a fight with your wife/girlfriend? Did you lose your job? Can you afford to buy back into the bracket race if you lose this round? All of these items (and many more) can emotionally impact your thoughts and allow your mind to be somewhere besides devoting complete attention to reaction times. While you may not be able to correct these conditions that are affecting your mental state it is good for you to be aware that they can impair your reaction times. Just before you stage the car try to clear your mind of any negative thoughts and concentrate on the tree only.

Conditions relating to sunlight and tree visibility can also affect you. What time of day is it? What direction is the track positioned? Is it a daytime or nighttime race? Are the bulbs incandescent or LED? Reaction times decrease as the sky becomes darker. There are also sunglasses designed to filter out surrounding yellows and make the yellow bulbs on the tree stand out more and decrease your reaction time.

Many things affect your physical reaction time and can be improved upon. Do you exercise? Did you get enough sleep? Is your overall health good? Is your vision the best?

Dick Miller making another run in the mid 10s with his 3,800-pound Cutlass. Notice how level the front end is with both tires the same level off the ground, planting the rear tires evenly. Just enough weight transfer (pitch rotation) and lift in the rear to push those wrinkle-wall tires into the pavement. The tread is very flat for as much traction as possible. Notice also that both rear tires have the same number of wrinkles.

wheel stand? Any time a car lifts in the front (since it is rotating on the rear tires) it is actually moving the front of the car rearward before it can go forward. So, are wheelie bars necessary or (if you have them already) should they be adjusted? Should you launch at a lower RPM to limit the power going to the tires? If the front wheels come off the ground more than about 1 foot, it's counterproductive.

Torque Converter

How loose or tight the torque converter is affects reaction time. You need to find out the answers to a few questions and make the appropriate adjustments. Is the torque converter matching up to your particular engine needs? Does the converter have to much slip before starting to move the car? Is it out of the maximum power band?

Front Tires

Front tire circumference, as well as tire pressure, greatly affects tire rollout and where you position the car on the track.

Shorter tires give quicker reaction times because a smaller circumference gives less roll out and a slower ET. Taller tires give slower reaction times because a larger circumference gives more roll out and a faster ET.

The same size tire can be made to appear larger or smaller by adjusting the tire pressure. Less air gives the tire more of a flat look, which makes the footprint larger and tricks the photocells into thinking it is much larger than it is. Likewise, more air makes the tire much stiffer making the photocell think the tire is much smaller than it is.

Rear Tires

Rear tire traction doesn't only affect 60-foot times, but also reaction times. Just because tires have measurable tire tread doesn't mean they are still good. If your tires are not near new and your 60-foot times and reaction times start to slow down or vary, you probably are in need of new tires no matter how much tread is left.

The First 60 Feet

Are your car's ETs inconsistent? Take a look at the 60-foot times. There is a photocell and reflector set (just like at the starting line) exactly 60 feet from the starting line. This clocking can tell you a lot about the run. Normally a variation in the

60-foot time creates two to three times as much difference in the overall ET. Ideally the 60-foot time should be the same from run to run with perhaps .002 to .003 second of variance. Cars varying more than .02 to .03 second have an issue that needs to be addressed.

Many things can affect 60-foot times. The most important is that the clockings are identical from run to run. And even if they are, you may still wonder if they are right.

For testing, 60-foot times must be compared with runs using exactly the same launch (tire pressure, tire diameter, engine speed, stage at the same spot, etc.). When you leave the starting line in relation to the light has no bearing on the 60-foot clocking. The 60-foot clocking measures only the time from when you left the starting line to when you broke the 60-foot beam.

What can affect 60-foot times? Just about everything!

Assuming you have no mismatch of components; enough fuel pressure; a good tune on the engine, carburetor, and distributor; a good transmission; and a good rear end (either locked or positraction), your 60-foot times should be very consistent. If not, you need to look at the tires and your burnout methods. If your car's 60-foot times were consistent when you installed your tires and have since become inconsistent, it may be time to look at new tires.

MPH	1/4 ET	1/8 ET	60 FEET	MPH	1/4 ET	1/8 ET	60 FEET
92.80	14.00	9.00	1.85	141.60	9.50	6.01	1.31
94.80	13.75	8.83	1.82	146.80	9.25	35.85	1.28
96.70	13.50	8.66	1.79	151.20	9.00	5.69	1.25
98.70	13.25	8.49	1.76	156.00	8.75	5.53	1.22
100.40	13.00	8.32	1.73	160.80	8.50	5.37	1.19
102.30	12.75	8.15	1.70	165.60	8.25	5.21	1.16
104.20	12.50	7.98	1.67	170.40	8.00	5.05	1.13
106.80	12.25	7.81	1.64	176.40	7.75	4.90	1.10
109.50	12.00	7.64	1.61	182.40	7.50	4.74	1.07
112.20	11.75	7.47	1.58	188.70	7.25	4.59	1.04
115.00	11.50	7.30	1.55	195.10	7.00	4.43	1.01
118.00	11.25	7.14	1.52	203.70	6.75	4.27	0.98
121.00	11.00	6.98	1.49	212.30	6.50	4.12	0.95
123.50	10.75	6.81	1.46	220.90	6.25	3.96	0.92
126.00	10.50	6.65	1.43	230.00	6.00	3.81	0.89
130.20	10.25	6.49	1.40	243.70	5.75	3.66	0.86
134.50	10.00	6.33	1.37	257.40	5.50	3.49	0.83
138.10	9.75	6.17	1.34				

You can use this 60-foot chart as a guide. Take a look at the 1/4-mile ET column (or if you are running 1/8-mile, use the 1/8-mile ET column). Find your typical average ET. Then, look across to the right and find the suggested 60-foot clocking for that ET. If you are way over that 60-foot time, you may need to work on getting the car to move that first 60 feet quicker. You can also look at the MPH column to see if your car is as quick as it should be for the top speed it runs. If not, look again at the 60-foot time and you may see the reason.

Choosing The Right Torque Converter

If you don't have the opportunity to dyno-test your engine, it is still very easy to pick out the right torque converter for your combination. When building a race car three things must match, functioning together: the intake, camshaft, and torque converter.

An intake manifold and camshaft are usually advertised with the recommended engine speed. If you install a cam that makes power from 3,000 to 6,000 rpm, you need an intake manifold that starts making power about 2,500 to 3,000 rpm. The torque converter needs to stall at about 3,000 to 3,500 rpm.

It is absolutely critical that these three items match. If you have any doubts, your camshaft sales person can help you determine the right parts.

Starting-Line Ratio

If the tires are good, another factor often overlooked is the starting-line ratio. The starting-line ratio is a combination of the first-gear transmission ratio multiplied by the rear-end gear ratio. A relatively narrow-tired car (each rear tire measures 11 inches or less across the tread) has a certain maximum starting-line ratio to be used based upon the weight of the car and the stroke of the engine. The stroke of an engine determines the possible torque that engine should generate.

Starting-Line Ratio =
First-Gear Ratio x Rear-Axle Gear Ratio

For example, if your car's transmission has a 2.48:1 first-gear ratio and a 4.10:1 rear-axle gear ratio, the starting-line ratio is 10.168:1.

If you have a 3,500-pound car

Stroke	Weight (pounds)							
(inches)	1,000	1,500	2,000	2,500	3,000	3,500	4,000	4,500
2.75	11.00	11.25	11.50	11.75	12.00	12.25	12.50	12.75
2.88	10.75	11.00	11.25	11.50	11.75	12.00	12.25	12.50
3.00	10.50	10.75	11.00	11.25	11.50	11.75	12.00	12.25
3.13	10.25	10.50	10.75	11.00	11.25	11.50	11.75	12.00
3.25	10.00	10.25	10.50	10.75	11.00	11.25	11.50	11.75
3.38	9.75	10.00	10.25	10.50	10.75	11.00	11.25	11.50
3.50	9.50	9.75	10.00	10.25	10.50	10.75	11.00	11.25
3.63	9.25	9.50	9.75	10.00	10.25	10.50	10.75	11.00
3.75	9.00	9.25	9.50	9.75	10.00	10.25	10.50	10.75
3.88	8.75	9.00	9.25	9.50	9.75	10.00	10.25	10.50
4.00	8.50	8.75	9.00	9.25	9.50	9.75	10.00	10.25
4.13	8.25	8.50	8.75	9.00	9.25	9.50	9.75	10.00
4.25	8.00	8.25	8.50	8.75	9.00	9.25	9.50	9.75
4.38	7.75	8.00	8.25	8.50	8.75	9.00	9.25	9.50
4.50	7.50	7.75	8.00	8.25	8.50	8.75	9.00	9.25
4.63	7.25	7.50	7.75	8.00	8.25	8.50	8.75	9.00
4.75	7.00	7.25	7.50	7.75	8.00	8.25	8.50	8.75
4.88	6.75	7.00	7.25	7.50	7.75	8.00	8.25	8.50
5.00	6.50	6.75	7.00	7.25	7.50	7.75	8.00	8.25

Multiply the car's rear-end ratio times the transmission first-gear ratio to come up with a starting-line ratio. This chart is based upon engine stroke (torque) and car weight and tells you if the car is over-geared, under-geared, or just right.

with a crankshaft stroke of 3.75 inches, you are very close to your ideal starting-line ratio. If you have a 3,000-pound car with a 4.50-inch crankshaft stroke, the ideal starting-line ratio is 8.5:1. Your car's starting-line ratio of 10.168:1 is too high, and will likely overpower the tires. Also, the car will tend to be very inconsistent.

How do you correct your starting-line ratio? First, it is not impossible to make the above scenario work, but to do so you have to somehow remove power from the car at the starting line. This can be accomplished in many ways. Here are a few ideas to try without changing the rear axle gears.

If you have a car with a computer-controlled power-adder (with nitrous oxide, for example), you should have the option to reduce the power at the starting line and bring in full power down track. If it is a non-computer-controlled power adder (like a turbo or supercharger), you may have to reduce the boost pressure, which ultimately reduces the overall power.

If it is a non-power-adder car, you can use a switch and reduce the timing in first gear only.

While these suggestions may help, they all reduce power, which slows the car. However, if the car is overpowering the tires, it could run faster if it hooks harder and leaves quicker and more consistently.

MSD makes a programmable ignition system that allows the user to set the distributor timing curve to any specification with a laptop computer. This allows for timing retard at the

starting line and then brings it back in at the rate desired. This MSD box also has a great feature that allows you to independently set engine RPM limits for the water burnout, the launch (if using a transmission brake), and the upper (safety) RPM to prevent over-revving the engine.

Another way to correct your starting-line ratio is to change the rear-end gear ratio. This affects the entire acceleration process and is permanent, but again if the car is over-powering the rear tires it may hook harder and leave quicker, producing a quicker ET.

If you feel you have the correct rear-gear ratio (based on reaching the engine's maximum horsepower RPM at the finish line), another way to correct the problem would be to change the transmission to one with a lower first-gear ratio, and leave the rear-end gear ratio untouched.

For instance, back to our example: If you change the transmission first-gear ratio from a 2.48:1 to a 2.10:1, the car's starting line ratio is now 8.61:1 (2.1 x 4.10). This is ideal for the same 3,000-pound car with a 4.5-inch-stroke engine.

Once you are past the 60-foot point, the rest of the run should be very simple. Just one or two shifts, hit the brakes after crossing the finish line, and stop at the ET shack, pick up your time slip and return to the pits.

Dissecting The Run

On page 112 is a typical timeslip. Let's look it over, and discuss what it says and means.

The reaction time (R/T) of .514 indicates that the car left the starting line .014 second after the green light came on.

The 60-foot beam was broken 1.492 seconds later.

The 330-foot beam was broken 4.403 seconds later.

The car broke the eighth-mile beam in 6.851 seconds, traveling at 100.21 mph.

The 1,000-foot beam was broken 8.894 seconds after leaving the starting line, and the quarter-mile was finished in 10.794 seconds, traveling at 124.58 mph.

Refer to the 60-foot chart on page 110 and analyze the run. In the

```
Car # 5867

Dial
R/T        ….514
60-foot  …1.492
330        …4.403
1/8        …6.851
MPH      …100.21
1000      …8.894
1/4        …10.794
MPH      …124.58
```

At the top of the slip on the left side (if you ran the left lane; on the right side if you ran the right lane) is your car number.

quarter-mile column we find the ET closest to the 10.794 on our ET slip. The 10.75 indicates that our 60-foot time should be 1.46, or .032 faster than recorded. The 10.75-second row also indicates that our eighth-mile should be 6.81, or .041 faster than the 6.851 that was recorded. The suggested MPH for a 10.75 pass indicates that the MPH should be 123.5, or 1.08 mph slower than recorded.

What this ET slip says is that from the start, the 60-foot time was not the best for that ET, resulting in a run slower than the chart and with more MPH than the chart. The car's launch is not optimized. The high speed (MPH) at the finish line indicates the horsepower the engine is making. Looking at the chart again, you could calculate that the MPH would have been good for a 10.642-second run, had the 60-foot been what it should have been.

$$126.0 - 123.5 = 2.5$$
$$126.0 - 124.58 = 1.42$$

$$1.42 \div 2.5 = .568$$
$$10.75 - 10.5 = .25$$
$$2.5 \times .568 = .142 + 10.5 = 10.642$$

Every fraction of a second reduced from the 60-foot time typically reduces the ET by two to three times as much. So, if you take the .032 second that the 60-foot was off, and multiply it by 3, you get .096 second. When we subtract that from the quarter-mile ET of 10.794, you get 10.698. This is still not perfect, according to the chart, but you can see how to use it to analyze the ET slip.

If the car was running an eighth-mile pass, take the .032 second the 60-foot was off by, and multiply it by 2 (which equals .064 second). Subtract that from the eighth ET of 6.851 seconds, and you get 6.787 seconds compared to the chart recommendation of 6.81.

How is MPH recorded when there are no police standing on the track with radar guns? The track MPH is calculated by the time it takes to travel from a photocell and reflector set exactly 66 feet before the eighth-mile photocell. The same is true at the quarter-mile finish line.

Prior to 1989, it was calculated by the time it took to travel 66 feet before the eighth-mile or quarter-mile photocell and reflector set to another set 66 feet after the eighth-mile or quarter-mile finish line, or 132 feet total. Since most drivers are on the brakes immediately after the finish line, a false MPH (slow) is recorded.

Comparing Runs

I strongly suggest keeping track of your runs using a logbook. This is a good way to keep your ETs in order

A good log book is necessary to keep track of weather changes and/or mechanical changes and how they effect the car. Finding similar circumstances will tell you where your cars ET should be that day.

by date. A logbook can not only allow you to keep track of your ET slips, but also factors like the weather conditions, tire pressure, carburetor settings, and the number of runs on key items. When testing changes or comparing tuning results, these notes become very valuable in determining which factors contributed to your gains and/or losses.

After reading this chapter you should be able to analyze your burnout, reaction time, 60-foot time, and ET slip. Using your analysis and making appropriate adjustments where needed, you should be well on your way to becoming a more consistent and winning driver.

		Date			Event				
	1	2	3	4	5	6	7	8	9
Day of week									
Time of day									
Lane									
TT/Elim									
Dial in									
Reaction									
60'									
Split 60-330									
330'									
Split 330-660									
660'									
660 MPH									
Split 660-1000									
1000'									
1000 MHP									
Split 1000-1320									
1320'									
1320 MPH									
Barometer									
Temp									
Humidity									
Density									
Correction									
ADR									
Tire press									
Tires									
Front Shock									
Rear Shock									
Jets									
Squirters									
Shift									
Runs on plugs									
Runs on tires									
Runs on engine									
Runs on Trans									
Runs on T/C									
Notes									
Notes									
Notes									

Keeping track of changes in the car or weather helps you analyze the car's performance later. Also, keeping track of the runs on tires, plugs, etc., helps you decide on preventive maintenance measures.

SUGGESTIONS FOR A MORE CONSISTENT AND WINNING CAR

At the beginning of my 40-plus years of drag racing, someone with a fairly consistent car and good starting-line reflexes could win his or her share of drag races as I did on national, state, and local levels. When I first started drag racing 60-foot clocks did not exist. I can even remember running time-trials four cars wide. As the years passed, new things were developed to level the playing field. Even 40 years (and many different cars) later, I still win races and track championships in the same car I started in, but times have changed.

This chapter discusses several ideas for making your car more consistent. The more consistent your car is, the more races you can win. A consistent car also allows for more accurate data when testing new combinations and therefore a faster car. You may already have many of them on your car and you may have heard of others but have not given them much thought.

One of the advantages of running one car for more than 40 years (even though I have had many others) is that I have tried almost every product on the market and know what works and what doesn't. I have tried many things that I quickly got rid of because they just didn't work as advertised. Other times there was something else out there claiming to be better, and I wanted to try it instead. As a result of all this experimenting, I have found eight things

(in no particular order) that I feel every bracket racer should have. If you look at the racers who win, they are already incorporating these exact ideas, or something similar. Gone are the days of a good driver winning on his skills alone.

Don't misunderstand me. Experience helps make the right decisions

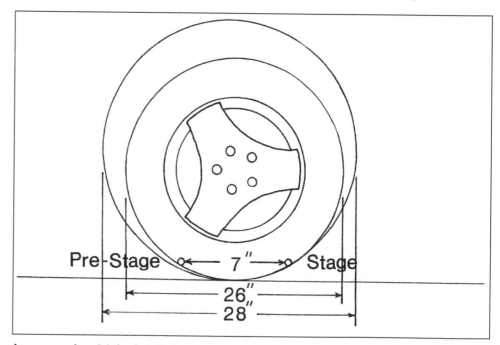

In comparing 26-inch tall tires with 28-inch tall tires, the difference in rollout distance can be seen. You can use this difference to your advantage if you take it into account when staging the car.

but knowledge and information help take the guesswork out of those decisions.

Tall Tires

The correct-diameter front tires for the best 60-foot times and best reaction-time combinations are different for every driver and car combination. The same things hold true for either foot-brake cars or transbrake-equipped cars. Tire diameter can adjust your 60-foot times, but also affects your reaction times, so you need to compromise to achieve the best-possible front tire for you and your car. Since it is hard to adjust the driver sometimes, a different-diameter front tire is the best way. The taller tire has more of a rollout (larger circumference) and therefore the better your 60-foot clockings are.

Mickey Thompson front tires with a 26-inch diameter have a rollout of 78 inches. The same tire in a 28-inch diameter has a rollout of 86 inches. Unless you are deep staged (staging enough forward that the pre-stage light goes out), normally your front tires have the leading edge of the tire breaking the staged beam (photocell) while the trailing edge is still breaking the pre-staged beam.

With 7 inches between the stage beam and the pre-staged beam, the tire is able to roll at least 7 inches more before leaving the stage beam and activating the red light. If your front tire has a circumference of 86 inches, it is able to roll farther than a tire with a 78-inch circumference. Not only is your car able to move the 7 inches, but it also gains the distance provided by any amount of tire diameter still left in the pre-stage beam as you are breaking the stage beam.

This is like a rolling start! With the larger-diameter tire having more distance before exiting the pre-stage beam, the 60-foot time is quicker than for the same car with smaller-diameter tires. The same holds true for the rest of the times recorded farther down the track.

Reaction time is based on the actual time from when you exit the staged beam and the light turns red or green. Therefore, if you have a taller tire the 60-foot times (rolling start) are quicker, but your reaction time is slower due to the longer roll-out required before the tire exits the staged beam.

Normally, for winning races, I say go for the best-possible reaction time. In bracket racing, it's not how fast you get there but how consistently you get there coupled with a great reaction time.

The whole picture can become very complicated. Let's say you have the right tire (usually the tallest tire) for your best 60-foot times ever, but your reaction time needs to improve. One quick thing to look at is front-tire air pressure. Lower front-tire air pressure creates a longer rollout, and higher front tire pressure creates a shorter rollout.

Likewise, less front-tire air pressure creates a larger footprint, meaning there is more tire left in the pre-stage beam for a quicker 60-foot time and a slower reaction time. Higher front tire air pressure creates a smaller footprint, meaning there is less tire left in the pre-stage beam for a slower 60-foot time and a quicker reaction time. I have even seen cars with one side tire-and-suspension assembly removed and reattached farther rearward to create a much longer rollout.

Accelerator linkage can be adjusted as well; not only at the pedal but also at the carburetor. Be sure the engine responds as quickly as possible when you press down on the gas pedal.

The race cars of today have more and more electronics than cars of the past, including the possibility of electronically controlled shifters, transmission brakes, shock adjusters, programmable ignitions, data recorders, and more. I refer to them that way (cars of the past) because most drag race cars of today are cars of the past no matter how modified they may be. While it is not unusual to see a car run 9.50-second ETs, that was what a Pro/Stock car ran 40 years ago. There are many reasons for these advancements, but almost all of them besides tires (see Chapter 9) need more and better electronics to utilize these new improvements.

Remember, no one single combination fits all. It is up to you to see what would make you and your car the best winning combination possible by working on your reaction time and 60-foot time.

Power Saving

Most race cars today run an alternator to be sure the battery is in the best condition possible for each run, all the way through the run. Unless you enjoy charging your car's battery between runs, at the very minimum you should go to a 12-volt alternator such the one-wire units available from Powermaster that generate 70 amps at idle. That means not only is the alternator charging the battery going down track, but also while on the return road and while idling in the pits or staging lanes, or any time the engine is running.

Being from the old school, old habits die hard. After changing to a one-wire Powermaster alternator, I still charged my battery between rounds. I like to double-enter some races, which means there is even less time between rounds. So I bought a voltmeter, and by monitoring it between rounds I found it wasn't necessary to charge my car's battery between rounds, or even at all. I use a 12-volt battery tender between events to be sure the battery is at full charge before the next race.

For experimental purposes, I recently installed an XS Power 16-volt absorbed glass mat (AGM) maintenance-free battery and corresponding Powermaster 16-volt alternator. I expected to see a safety margin in reserve voltage available at the track between rounds. What I also got (and didn't expect) was all my electrically-powered accessories (including the cooling fans,

water pump, and fuel pump) ran at a higher RPM. They were all noticeably faster and I could hear the difference. My engine (with 509 ci and 12.5:1 compression) starts quite hard on occasion; especially after it has some heat in it, and sometimes it kicks back against the starter.

With this setup, it sounds like a completely different engine when turning over. The starter spins it over so effortlessly it sounds like the car has no spark plugs. Since I still carry my battery in the stock location, I bought a new battery tray and hold-down fabricated that bolts right into the factory spot. Of course, a 16-volt battery charger is needed to keep 16-plus volts in the battery. When fully charged, the battery should hold 19.2 volts.

AGM batteries have high cold-cranking amperages and hold a charge for a much longer time. There is no liquid acid in an AGM battery. They never need liquid added, are maintenance-free, are non-spillable, and they can be mounted in any angle except completely upside-down.

They do contain vents which are normally closed, but should the battery be overcharged and internal pressure build up, the vents open to release it. This is a very rare occurrence;

This is an XS Power 16-volt AGM battery. They never require maintenance and offer higher voltage levels to crank over high-compression racing engines with relative ease. They also last longer than traditional flooded-cell batteries, and don't require a perfectly level mounting. Competing AGM batteries made by other manufacturers offer similar benefits, but I've had good luck with the XS Power product.

Switching from a 12-volt battery to a 16-volt battery also requires a 16-volt alternator like this one from Powermaster.

Here is a typical Powermaster high-performance alternator. Other manufacturers offer similar products, but I choose Powermaster after many years of using them without issues. The company's wide range of products means it should have an alternator to replace a factory unit directly and offer improved charging potential.

The 16-volt battery from XS Power does not have all the same hold-downs as some factory batteries. I contacted Advanced Chassis to make me a new bolt-in battery tray.

however, and today's maintenance-free AGM batteries are highly recommended, as they are better in every way than the traditional flooded lead-acid batteries they replace.

Another area of importance for saving power is the starter. I run a Powermaster XS Torque Starter. Not only does it take up less space (giving me more header clearance) but with its aluminum case, it weighs only 8 pounds—about half the weight of a normal heavy-duty starter.

Remember, less weight means quicker ETs. Research has shown that 100 pounds equals approximately .10 second in ET. By being smaller in size and farther away from the engine block and exhaust headers, the starter doesn't soak up as much heat. Therefore, its tolerances are maintained much better and it starts the engine more easily when the engine temperature is higher, raising compression. It has 200 ft-lbs of cranking power and uses a 4.4:1 gear reduction design to be able to get the job done, even with engines pushing up to 18:1 compression ratio.

Shifter Style

One of the things that helps my car run so consistently is the shifter. The last time I raced, it ran 7.04, 7.04, 7.03, and 7.03 in the late afternoon and early evening. Over the years, I have used many shifters ranging from the factory style to the aftermarket ratchet style to electrically-activated units and air-shifted units. The Precision Performance Products shifter provides solid movement of the shifter at exactly the same RPM for both shifts, time after time. And it looks good.

The model I am using is a reverse pattern. It is triggered by an MSD RPM switch and is operated by a carbon dioxide bottle. Like everything else, I felt I needed a backup carbon dioxide bottle, which is a good idea, but I have been using this shifter for well over a year now on the same bottle. It can be used for standard- or manual-valve bodies, with forward or reverse patterns, and is complete with a neutral safety starting switch, a reverse lockout switch, and a transmission brake switch.

Transmission Brake

Even though I run in the the foot-brake class, I like having a transmission brake. The good thing about a transmission brake switch is that if you roll into the staged beam too far and wish to back up (which is typically not allowed) and your competitor is already pre-staged, you can simply put the shifter into neutral, hit the transmission brake button, and the car is in reverse. You can back up and quickly shift back into first gear, usually before anyone even knows what happened. It's much quicker and easier than shifting into neutral, pressing the reverse lockout button, shifting into reverse, backing up, shifting into neutral, and then shifting back into first.

Weather Stations

Weather stations have gotten more affordable over the years. When I first started racing, all that was available were temperature, humidity, and barometer gauge sets. By recording

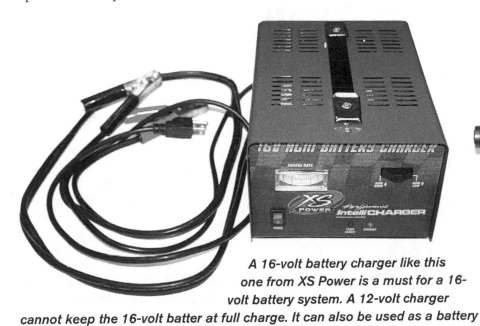

A 16-volt battery charger like this one from XS Power is a must for a 16-volt battery system. A 12-volt charger cannot keep the 16-volt batter at full charge. It can also be used as a battery maintainer between races, lengthening the life of the battery.

High-torque starters like this one from Powermaster are capable of starting engines with 19:1 compression and are reliable start after start. They also run cooler due to more header clearance.

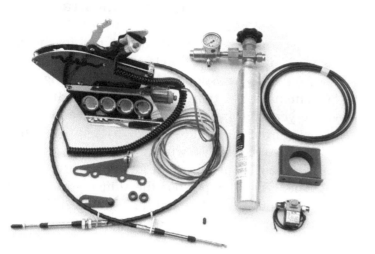

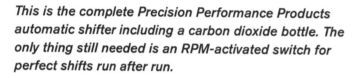

This is the complete Precision Performance Products automatic shifter including a carbon dioxide bottle. The only thing still needed is an RPM-activated switch for perfect shifts run after run.

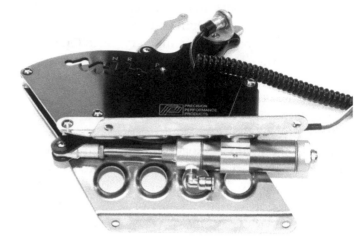

This Precision Performance Products shifter has an air-controlled actuator underneath the actual shifter. A shot of air from the RPM-activated switch opens the air solenoid and provides a momentary shot of air to the actuator and moves the shifter into another position.

old runs and the gauge settings you could fairly predict your next run's ET or dial-in. The old seat of the pants or just experience worked great also if there were no changes in the weather but should a weather front come through, without consulting any gauges, your ET would probably change and you could be on the trailer wondering why.

Back then local track bracket points chases were pretty well a weekly affair. Such experience pretty well separated the every week racers from the under experienced once in a while racers. Changes in the quality of air (density) not only could slow down or possibly speed up a car but also might require a change in fuel mixture.

Air density gauges came later in the 1980s. Air density decreases with increasing altitude as does barometric air pressure. It can also change with changes in temperature and/or humidity. The less dense the air, the less power your engine makes and the slower the ET. Also, less oxygen is present in less dense air so you will need to adjust your fuel mixture to a leaner condition. Air density depends on temperature, barometric pressure, and how much humidity is in the air. If an engine was at optimum air/fuel mixture while in denser air and less dense air moved in, the engine could be in an over-rich condition. This

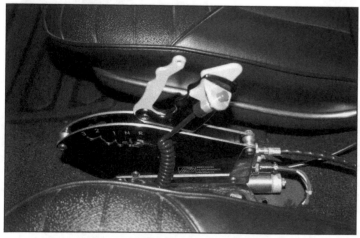

The Precision Performance Products shifter installed very neatly between the seats of a 1970 Cutlass W-31.

This RPM-activated switch from MSD plugs into the MSD box and uses RPM chips to control when to provide carbon dioxide to the shifter. If you want to change shift RPM, just change to another chip.

Be sure you mount the carbon dioxide bottle in a secure and upright position and somewhere you can reach it without too much trouble for that time when you just remembered you forgot to turn it on for the day's activities.

could create a condition anywhere from not noticeable to seeing black smoke coming out of the exhaust upon acceleration.

While this is not necessarily harmful to your engine for a short time, if severe enough, this may fowl out the spark plugs which will add to the power loss. Changing the fuel back to its optimum mixture you gain back some of the power lost. You can't do anything in a naturally aspirated engine (no power adder) to ever get back all 100 percent of the power lost in less dense air. If the air becomes more dense then the car can make more power. Due to the denser air you must richen your car's fuel mixture back to optimum air/fuel

An air density gauge can help you when recording runs in your log book.

mixture, which will make even more power.

However, not richening back to optimum air/fuel mixture causes a lean condition. Depending upon how drastic the air density has changed, this could show as a pulsating miss at the top end of the track or a bog off the starting line. Over lean conditions can over a period of time burn pistons, rings, and/or valves thus making for a very expensive repair.

A race car's engine is an air pump and a naturally aspirated (no power adders) engine can only pump a certain volume of air. The density of that air can dictate how much power that engine can make.

Barometric Pressure and Air Density

Increasing barometric pressure increases the density. Using an air storage tank as an example, if it contains 20 pounds of air pressure and you add more air to the same tank the pressure will increase corresponding to the amount of air you add yet it is still in the same size container. Since a race car's engine is an air pump, denser air being pumped into

the cylinders needs a richer mixture, therefore making more power.

Lower barometric air pressure creating less dense air needs a leaner mixture, therefore making less power. Altitude and barometric pressure can both change the air density. As you go higher in altitude, such as in the mountains in Denver, the air density decreases just as going to sea level or lower will cause an increase in air density. Weather changes can change the barometric pressure either higher or lower and will also affect the air's density, but not nearly as much as altitude.

Barometric pressure is higher on a nice cool sunny day, meaning denser air. If an afternoon storm comes in the barometric pressure will lower as will the air density. The barometric pressure again increases raising the air density as the storm passes. Therefore, air density is at its lowest at a high elevation on a hot day when the barometric pressure is low. The air's density is highest at low elevations when the barometric pressure is high and the temperature is low.

Temperature and Air Density

Temperature has the opposite effect on air density as does barometric pressure. Using a balloon as an example, heating the air captured in a balloon expands the balloon just as cooling it causes it to shrink. However, the same hot air not in a balloon (surrounded by nothing but air) pushes the surrounding air aside.

As a result, the amount of air in a particular area decreases when the air is heated if the air is not captured as in a balloon. In normal atmosphere the air's density decreases as the air is heated. This makes less power and requires a leaner fuel mixture change

Higher air barometric readings mean denser air and more power, indicating a possible leaner engine condition. The same in reverse if the barometric reading gets lower.

Lower air temperature means denser air and more power, indicating a leaner engine condition. The same in reverse if the air gets warmer.

Lower humidity readings indicate denser air and more power, indicating a leaner engine condition. The same in reverse if the humidity gets higher.

due to the less oxygen available with the less dense air. Likewise the air's density increases as the air is cooled. This makes more power and requires a richer fuel mixture change due to the more oxygen available with the more dense air.

Humidity and Air Density

Even though I explain how humidity effects air density I am not sure it has the power-robbing effect on performance you might expect as with barometric pressure and temperature. Humidity (vaporized water) when mixed with an exploding charge of a fuel and air mixture will explode itself, and create steam which being in a confined space will also help to develop horsepower.

Humid air is less dense than dry air. Scientists explain that a fixed volume of gas, let's say 1 cubic foot, at the same temperature and pressure, always has the same number of molecules no matter what gas is in the container. Imagine a cubic foot of perfectly dry air. It contains about 78 percent nitrogen molecules, with

each molecule having a molecular weight of 28. Another 21 percent of the air is oxygen, with each molecule having a molecular weight of 32. Molecules are free to move in and out of that 1 cubic foot of air.

What scientist lead us to conclude is that if we added water vapor molecules to that 1 cubic foot of air, some of the nitrogen and oxygen molecules would leave (remember the total number of molecules in one cubic foot of air stays the same at the same temperature and pressure). The water molecules, which replace nitrogen or oxygen, have a molecular weight of 18. This is lighter than both nitrogen and oxygen. In other words, replacing nitrogen and oxygen with water vapor decreases the weight of the air in the cubic foot and density decreases. Compared to the differences made by temperature and air pressure, humidity has a small effect on the air's density. But, humid air is lighter than dry air at the same temperature and pressure.

Isn't water heavier than air? If you pour water in a bucket doesn't

it go to the bottom with the air on top? This is true in a liquid form. But, the water that makes the air humid isn't liquid. It's water vapor, which is a gas that is lighter than nitrogen or oxygen. When humidity reaches 100 percent it is then a liquid falling from the sky to the bottom of the bucket. Humidity is measured as a percentage of the ratio of the current absolute humidity to the highest absolute humidity possible. This is water vapor that a given amount of air can contain with 100 percent being the maximum amount before it returns to a liquid state and falls out of the sky as rain. Humidity doesn't have to be at 100 percent at ground level before rain can occur but it must be 100 percent somewhere in the clouds above the earth.

A reading of 100 percent relative humidity means that the air is totally saturated with water vapor and cannot hold any more, creating the possibility of rain. The amount of water vapors the atmosphere can hold before reaching 100 percent depends upon on the current air temperature.

Warmer air can evaporate more water vapors than cooler air. Thus, on any given day if the temperature rises the humidity level will decrease. As the cool night air comes in the same amount of water vapors in the air will give a higher humidity reading. Therefore, with the cooler night air and the same amount of water in the air the humidity will read higher yet more power is available because the cooler denser air now has more molecules. Since the water molecules are the same number there will be more oxygen and nitrogen molecules even with a higher humidity reading.

While we are talking about air density also consider that denser air will slow down objects moving through it more than less dense air because the object has to shove aside heavier molecules. Such air resistance is called "drag," which increases with air density. Cool, dense air creating more drag will slow a muscle car's acceleration rate; however, the additional horsepower created with this denser air will compensate for the drag and accelerate the car faster. Turbochargers or superchargers are

Computech's Race Air Pro Weather Station complete with carrying case keeps you current as to weather changes, and expected ET based on those changes.

ways of increasing the density of the air going into an engine.

Years ago, I developed my own computer program that recorded run information and the air density for each run. Then, given the new air density, I could look up all runs with the same air density.

Predicting Dial-ins

Weather stations kept evolving into more sophisticated instruments. Not too many years ago at a very big NHRA race in Memphis, I made it to the final round. There was a storm coming in and it got cloudy and cooled off several degrees. My opponent did not have a weather station/ET predictor. He dialed his car quicker as I would have also done based upon the cooler air. I consulted my local weather station and it indicated that with the coming storm and lower barometric pressure the air had gotten worse. I dialed my car slower. I took home the Wally.

I use the Computech's RaceAir Pro Competition Weather Analyzer and computer. Notice the *and computer*, as they now predict dial-ins, calculate jetting changes needed, throttle stop timer settings, many mathematical calculations, are used as a calculator, and run completion calculations based on partial runs.

When turned on, the Computech analyzer shows from memory the weather station readings from the last time it was on. Press the sample button and the analyzer turns on the fan which draws fresh air through the unit to get the current readings. This takes a few minutes before it will read "Sampled Weather" indicating it has fresh information. I have noticed if you move it around while it is sampling the air it takes longer to perform the sampling. Do

not set it in the sun when sampling or near any other sources of heat such as your exhaust or even your own body heat.

Once the air has been sampled, it displays current temperature, humidity, barometer readings, correction factor, and air density, among many others. I record all of the settings after each run on the ET slip and in my log book for reference material. For predicting dial-ins the only numbers you need is the correction factor.

The higher the number the worse the air and the lower the correction number the better the air. Let's say at 13:36 you ran your last time trial flat out with no lifting, and ran a 6.8747. When you returned to the trailer the analyzer correction factor was 1.0331 (70.7 degrees – 30 percent – 29.49). Due to some track problems your first round of eliminations wasn't until 16:24 (2.48 hours later). Running a fresh sample before you head to the staging lanes the correction factor now reads 1.0368 (72.8 degrees – 30 percent – 29.47). Press the dial-in key and the analyzer asks for the old correction factor. You enter the 1.0331. Now the analyzer needs the old ET, so enter 6.8747. The analyzer now asks if you want to use the current correction factor of 1.0368.

If you don't, enter the desired correction factor. If you do, just press enter and the analyzer indicates based on your last run compared to the present air conditions that your run should be 6.883. This run would be more in the middle of the day when the temperature is normally higher, causing the car to slow down.

2-Speed vs. 3-Speed

There are exceptions to every rule, but drag race cars weighing less

---

For dedicated drag racing cars, the modern versions of the old GM Powerglide 2-speed transmissions (like this one from TCI) may be ideal. They are certainly strong—capable of handling more than 1,000 hp with ease. Their gear ratios can be tailored to best suit your vehicle's requirements. They are best used in lighter-weight vehicles, including dragsters.

This GM TH-400 transmission is from TCI, and is suitable for heavier cars. It can handle big power reliably, and various first-gear ratios are offered. This particular TH-400 has the desirable 2.10:1 first gear.

than 3,000 pounds and running an automatic transmission are better off with a 2-speed Powerglide transmission for consistency. This is because the Powerglide has a higher (lower numerically) first gear and the fact that only one shift is required instead of two. However, for cars weighing more than 3,000 pounds, the lower first-gear ratio of a Turbo-Hydramatic transmission is needed to get the extra weight to move from a standing start. Also, because of the lower first-gear ratio, the middle (second) gear is required to bridge the gap between the low first gear and third gear.

That seems pretty simple, and if that were all there was to it, it would be. Both transmissions have a final gear ratio of 1:1, so once in the final (top) gear, they both perform the same. The big difference is the first-gear ratio.

From the factory, a Powerglide transmission has either a 1.76:1 or 1.82:1 first gear. Different-ratio first-gear sets are now available (through TCI Automotive, JW Performance Transmissions, and others) for the

Powerglide transmission. The Turbo 400 transmission has a first gear of 2.48:1 and second gear of 1.48:1. What becomes the issue here is how you can overpower the rear tires with too much starting-line ratio.

Based upon the stroke of your engine, which predetermines the torque it is capable of, there is a given number that you don't want to exceed for the weight of the car. For example:

My car (with me in it) weighs about 3,800 pounds. My engine has a 4.5-inch stroke. According to the chart on page 111, a 3,800-pound car with a 4.5-inch-stroke engine should have a starting-line ratio of 8.90:1 (between 8.75 and 9.00:1).

However, when we take my first-gear ratio of 2.48:1 and multiply it by the rear-end ratio of 4.10, we get 10.17:1 for a starting-line ratio. To

Stroke	Weight (pounds)							
(inches)	1,000	1,500	2,000	2,500	3,000	3,500	4,000	4,500
2.75	11.00	11.25	11.50	11.75	12.00	12.25	12.50	12.75
2.88	10.75	11.00	11.25	11.50	11.75	12.00	12.25	12.50
3.00	10.50	10.75	11.00	11.25	11.50	11.75	12.00	12.25
3.13	10.25	10.50	10.75	11.00	11.25	11.50	11.75	12.00
3.25	10.00	10.25	10.50	10.75	11.00	11.25	11.50	11.75
3.38	9.75	10.00	10.25	10.50	10.75	11.00	11.25	11.50
3.50	9.50	9.75	10.00	10.25	10.50	10.75	11.00	11.25
3.63	9.25	9.50	9.75	10.00	10.25	10.50	10.75	11.00
3.75	9.00	9.25	9.50	9.75	10.00	10.25	10.50	10.75
3.88	8.75	9.00	9.25	9.50	9.75	10.00	10.25	10.50
4.00	8.50	8.75	9.00	9.25	9.50	9.75	10.00	10.25
4.13	8.25	8.50	8.75	9.00	9.25	9.50	9.75	10.00
4.25	8.00	8.25	8.50	8.75	9.00	9.25	9.50	9.75
4.38	7.75	8.00	8.25	8.50	8.75	9.00	9.25	9.50
4.50	7.50	7.75	8.00	8.25	8.50	8.75	9.00	9.25
4.63	7.25	7.50	7.75	8.00	8.25	8.50	8.75	9.00
4.75	7.00	7.25	7.50	7.75	8.00	8.25	8.50	8.75
4.88	6.75	7.00	7.25	7.50	7.75	8.00	8.25	8.50
5.00	6.50	6.75	7.00	7.25	7.50	7.75	8.00	8.25

Suggested first-gear ratio chart.

The key to making an automatic transmission live in a heavy car with a lot of power lies in fortifying it with beefy internal components (such as these TCI goodies, including a six-pinion planetary set and additional clutches) and keeping the transmission fluid cool.

correct the situation, I can change the rear-end gear ratio to something around 3.59:1 since 8.9 ÷ 2.48 = 3.59. However, that also changes second and third gears, and affects acceleration throughout the whole run.

The other option is to change the first-gear ratio in the transmission. Manufacturers such as TCI Automotive offer complete gear sets (or complete transmissions) with a first-gear ratio of 2.10:1. Now my starting-line ratio is 2.10 x 4.10, or 8.61:1, and I have corrected it without changing acceleration the rest of the way down the track.

Data Records

If you are a one-person crew, a data recorder is necessary. There are different types with many channels to record different events, but one that records both engine RPM and driveshaft RPM is adequate.

Keeping track of data during the run is a job for a data recorder, such as this Sportsman unit from Racepak. It monitors all your vehicle's critical functions on every pass and allows you to track performance from run-to-run. This makes it much easier to judge the gain (or loss) from tuning changes.

When looking around for a new one, I kept hearing the same thing from other racers: The Sportsman Data Recorder from Racepak was a great unit. I now have one, and (if you're willing to invest the time) it can provide a lot of valuable information. Weighing less than 1 pound, measuring about 6x4.5x1 inches, and mounted under the passenger seat, you'll never know it's there until you're ready to download some data to analyze.

It comes with software to install on your laptop. You can either connect it to your laptop (with a provided

The data is recorded onto this compact memory card, which is just like the ones used in modern digital cameras. Most newer desktop and laptop computers have ports these memory cards can be plugged directly into, making it easy to download all the information gathered. This cuts down on bulky cords and wires, and makes using a data recorder easy and effective.

cable into a serial port) or it has provisions for an SD memory card that can be plugged into the laptop directly. Mine records engine RPM, driveshaft RPM, battery voltage, and lateral g-force as well as acceleration g-force.

Samples of data can be recorded at up to 100 times per second.

I have the advantage of seeing more numbers on the screen associated with the graphs than printed here. Take a look at Graph A below; this tells me the car was a foot brake car idling at the light about 1,600 rpm. Once the accelerator was depressed toward the floor, it took .242 second for the torque converter to reach a stall speed of about 3,750

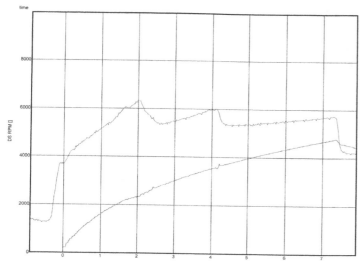

Graph A. This is a typical chart generated by the data recorder. It shows both engine RPM (top line) and driveshaft RPM (lower line), which allows you to see any radical changes between them. If the driveshaft RPM suddenly spikes, it's an indication of tire spin. This run was just about flawless, as driveshaft RPM gained steadily and both shifts were close to 6,000 rpm.

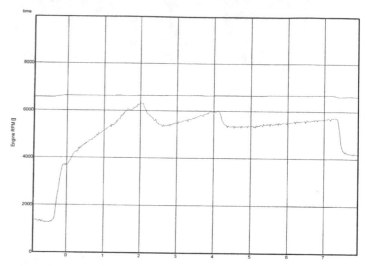

Graph B. Here's another chart courtesy of the data recorder. This one compares engine RPM (lower line) with system voltage throughout the run (upper line). As you can see, the electrical system maintained voltage steadily throughout the pass, proving the system is working just fine, as designed.

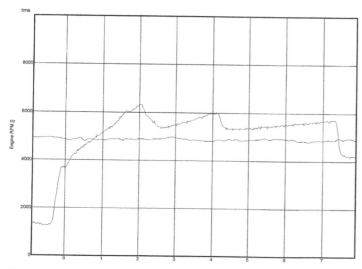

Graph C. Here's another engine RPM graph, this time compared to the lateral g-forces pushing the car from side-to-side. Obviously, this was a nice, straight pass. In a road racing car, the lateral g-loads increase dramatically around every turn.

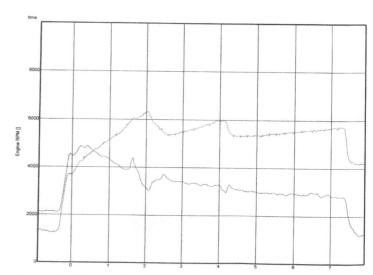

Graph D. This engine RPM g-load graph is for acceleration (lower line). It shows the harsh g-load pushing aft at the start, and settling down as the car accelerated. It picks up a bit at every gear change, and then relaxes again.

rpm. Part of that was time needed to fully depress the accelerator.

In another .112 second, the driveshaft began to move the car. The first- to second-gear shift was made at 6,320 rpm, while the second- to third-gear shift was made at 6,000 rpm, and I crossed the finish line at 5,671 rpm.

Since this is also a quarter-mile race car, it shouldn't cross the finish line at a higher engine RPM than the shift points. Even though the car was shifted at exactly 6,000 rpm on both shifts, the one-two shift is not as responsive as the two-three shift. Also at the one-two shift, it appears there was a little tire slippage shown in the driveshaft curve and even more in the two-three shift. How would I have known any of this without the data acquisition system telling me?

Looking at Graph B on page 124 you see there is no voltage drop at all. A consistent 13.2 volts were available throughout the entire run. My electrical system is working flawlessly.

When we look at the Graph C on page 124, it shows that the car has a little sideways motion, but

it's not bad. Perhaps it could be the front-end caster settings and not necessarily the rear tires. I'll monitor it in the future, and see if it's a consistent issue. If it becomes more pronounced, I'll know something is wearing out and requires service. If it goes away, I'll know it was a one-time occurrence.

Look at the Graph D on page 124. During the first .40 second of the run, an acceleration g-force of 1.40 was achieved and then steadily declined during the rest of the run. I can remember when I had my 1991 tube chassis-equipped Cutlass, the acceleration g-force was 2 to 2.4. The unit has to be mounted in a specific forward direction for the lateral and acceleration g-force meters to work properly.

Ignition System and RPM Limiters

Just as important as maintaining your battery to peak levels for operation of all electronics, you need an ignition system that is capable of delivering a high enough volt-

MSD's Programmable Digital 6AL-2 control box allows you to program in various RPM limiting functions for use at various places. The burnout RPM limit and an overall RPM limit are two good examples. This box is essential in a car with a manual transmission to avoid over-revving the engine.

age spark at all points throughout the run. Some ignition systems have extra capabilities besides just firing the spark plugs.

I run the MSD Programmable Digital 6AL box. There are other MSD boxes that can also perform the following functions. Using a serial-port-to-USB-port adapter cable (provided) you can connect the box to your laptop (if your computer does not have a USB port).

This MSD ignition box has three built-in RPM limiters. There is no more need for a multiple selection of RPM chips or rotary dials. One RPM limiter is to control the engine under wide-open throttle (WOT). Those who have ever lost a transmission or torque converter, missed a shift, or shifted into neutral all while under full throttle know the importance of an engine RPM limiter.

You simply select the RPM limit you want and enter the RPM at which you want the engine to be held. Since there is no need to run an engine past its peak-horsepower RPM, I would set the RPM limiter at 300 to 500 rpm above the peak horsepower point. If you have not dyno-tested your engine, I would set the RPM limiter at a similar 300 to 500 rpm above the highest engine speed obtained during your last run.

The second RPM limiter is only used when you are running a transmission brake. The RPM limiter holds the engine at your chosen speed while the trans brake button is engaged.

The third RPM limiter is my favorite, in that it limits the engine RPM during the burnout. It is tricky to maintain a steady RPM during a burnout while spinning the rear tires in water. With this RPM limiter being energized (along with the line lock)

MSD sells complete high-performance ignition systems designed to deal with the high RPM, heat, and abuse typical of racing. This particular kit includes everything from the distributor, coil, and spark plug wires to the programmable 6AL-2 box and additional RPM-activated switches. MSD offers complete kits like this for a wide range of engine families.

Trying this while running too much compression makes for a hard-starting engine. With the MSD Programmable Digital 6AL (a centrifugal advance but on your laptop) and your distributor curve mechanism locked out, set the timing at 4 degrees above where you intend to run it. Now you can set up the timing to always pull out 4 degrees of timing with your laptop.

If you are ever in a situation (such as poor weather) and wish to add up to 4 degrees of timing, it's simply a matter of plugging in your laptop and moving the timing line up however many degrees you wish.

You can also retard the timing further (14 degrees) for starting the engine. Although the engine has a heavier lope to the sound with the timing retarded and sounds cool, you have full advance back in at idle if you are a foot-brake racer and leave

all you need to do is hold your accelerator to the floor and make some smoke. I would also put the trans in high gear before the burnout to lessen the engine RPM needed to get some good heat into the tires.

Once you have completed the burnout, pull up to the line and pre-stage. I put the transmission in neutral and lightly rev it to be sure it is not loaded up with fuel. Then put the transmission in first gear and stage.

With today's ignitions, it probably isn't necessary to rev the engine, but what it does is ensure that after the burnout is completed in third gear, the car doesn't stage while still in third gear.

Another benefit of the MSD Programmable Digital 6AL box is you can program your entire distributor timing curve also from your laptop. Timing curves are very tricky to set and even sometimes once they are set they retard or take out timing at a high enough RPM when you don't expect it.

The best way to set your timing is to throw away your distributor's

mechanical weights and springs that control timing advance and lock out the curve completely. This can be accomplished differently on different distributors.

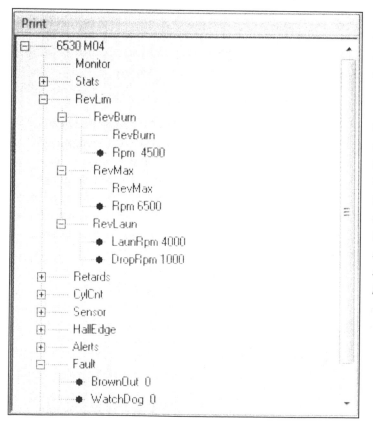

This screenshot shows the MSD RPM limits chart, as seen on a typical laptop. You can see the various RPM limiters and where they're set. Changing the limits is as easy as changing the numbers on the screen. If you're a serious racer, this is the way to go.

To give full timing control to the MSD computer, it's necessary to disable the mechanical timing advance mechanisms (weights and springs) from your traditional distributor. This is called "locking out" the distributor, and it's a fairly common and simple practice.

slow the first day. Then I speed it up for the second day (when you usually only get one time trial). That makes it hard for competitors who are really watching you to know what to expect from the car.

If you are running nitrous oxide, you can tie into the nitrous wiring so the box retards the timing instantly. Once you have all your settings where you want them, select "upload to the MSD box" on the screen, and that's all there is to it.

These are a few of the more important items that I have found over the years worth looking into. During an event, there are many things to keep track of and many decisions to be made. Of course experience helps, but the more data you have from your car, the better the decisions you can make. Strive to be consistent not only in your ET, but also in your staging and reaction times. Once you have accomplished this, you will win races.

the line at idle. If you are a transmission-brake racer, bring the timing to full advance at the RPM your engine sees while on the trans brake.

Either way, there is no lag time when you leave the starting line to when the engine sees full advance. You can download this software at MSD's Web site. This allows you to play with the software without making a purchase.

One of the things I have found

interesting with my MSD Programmable Digital 6AL, which I have never seen advertised, is you can use it to "dial-in a car." You can remove timing throughout the entire run and slow the car down. As a test I removed 20 degrees of timing and my car slowed down .50 second in the eighth-mile. It was as consistent at the slower time as it was at the normal time.

Sometimes when I go to a two-day event and race both days, I run it

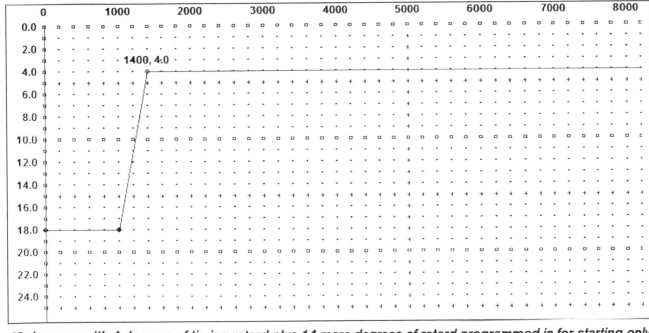

Here's another screen capture from the laptop. This one shows the timing advance program with a locked-out distributor in place. Note that the timing is set at 40 degrees, with 4 degrees of timing retard plus 14 more degrees of retard programmed in for starting only. Once the engine is started, all of the timing advance comes back in at 1,400 rpm. It sounds complicated, but it's much easier than wrestling with weights, springs, and vacuum advance cans like we used to.

Advanced Chassis
107 Victory Ln
Antwerp, OH 45813-8422
419-258-2100

Air Lift Company
2727 Snow Rd
Lansing, MI 48917
800-248-0892
www.airliftcompany.com

AJE Racing
6235 N Co Rd 275 W
North Vernon, IN 47265
800-877-7233
www.ajeracing.com

Allstar Performance Products
8300 Lane Dr
Watervliet, MI 49098
269-463-8000
www.allstarperformance.com

Broadus Automotive & Performance
3694 Cherry Rd
Memphis, TN 38118
901-366-7700

Calvert Racing Suspensions
4530 Runway Dr
Lancaster, CA 93536
661-728-9600
www.calvertracing.com

Computech Systems Inc
30071 Business Center Dr
Charlotte Hall, MD 20622
301-884-5712
www.computechracing.com

Dick Miller Racing
214 Sunrise Dr.
Science Hill, KY 42553
662-233-2301
www.dickmillerracing.com

Geezer Gassers
517 Maureen Dr
Eureka, MO 63025
636-938-9021
www.geezergassers.com

Harlow Racing Tires
1845 N Wayne Rd
Westland, MI 48185
734-722-7223
www.harlowracing.com

Hurst Racing Tires
P.O. Box 2818
Oregon City, OR 97045
503-656-1572
www.hurstracingtires.com

Landrum Spring
P.O. Box 337
Mentone, IN 46539
574-353-1674
866-703-3154
www.landrumspring.com

Lofgren Auto Sales
18130 Dahlia St NW
Cedar, MN 55011
763-753-7573
www.lofgrenauto.com

Longacre Racing Products Inc
16892 146th St SE
Monroe, WA 98272
800-423-3110
www.longacreracing.com

Mancini Racing
33524 Kelly Rd
Clinton Township, MI 48035
800-843-2821
www.manciniracing.com

Mickey Thompson Tires
4600 Prosper Dr
Stow, OH 44224
800-222-9092
www.mickeythompsontires.com

Moroso Performance
80 Carter Dr
Guilford, CT 06437
800-544-8894
www.moroso.com

MSD Ignition
1490 Henry Brennan Dr
El Paso, TX 79936
915-855-7123
www.msdignition.com

Powermaster Performance
1933 Downs Dr
West Chicago, IL 60185
www.powermasterperformance.com

Precision Performance Products
20122 State Rd
Cerritos, CA 90703
562-402-1108
www.precisionperformance.com

Racepak Data Systems
30402 Esperanza
Rancho Santa Margarita, CA 92688
949-709-5555
www.racepak.com

Scott Woerner
330 North McKenzie
Adrian, MI 49221
517-263-0239

Skinny Kid Race Cars
3170 E Oakley Park Rd, Suite A
Commerce Twp, MI 49390
248-668-1040
www.skinnykidracecars.com

Steeda Autosports
1351 Steeda Way
Pompano Beach, FL 33069
954-960-0774
www.steeda.com

TCI Automotive
151 Industrial Dr
Ashland, MS 38603
662-224-8972
www.tciauto.com

XS Power
2847 John Deere Dr, #102
Knoxville, TN 37917
888-497-7693
www.4xspower.com